# OUR SIXTH SENSE

Other books by J. M. Sanchez-Perez, M.D.

*Beliefs and Their Engrammes: Revised and Tested on the QE-2 World Cruise*

*Oppression, Violence and Repression*

*Babelism: Social Problems of the Watergate Era*

*The Hispanico*

*A Doctor's Odyssey*

# OUR SIXTH SENSE

## AN ORGANIC THEORY OF THE UNKNOWN

J. M. Sanchez-Perez, M.D.

Exposition Press Hicksville, New York

First Edition



ISBN 0-682-49072-5

Printed in the United States of America

# CONTENTS

# OUR SIXTH SENSE

# 1

# PARAPSYCHOLOGY

Today people have taken an interest in the sixth sense or, more correctly, in a number of psychic phenomena which in appearance have no relation to one another, sometimes defying logic and eluding any rational explanation. Included in this diverse realm are astrology, chiromancy, astral projection, hypnosis, telepathy, psychokinesis, psychic photography, and psychophony.

An increasing number of people believe that they have and do receive messages from the cosmic world. People seem to be strangely attracted by stories of the unknown, a fact which is verified by the unprecedented success of books and movies (such as *The Exorcist*) dealing with the occult. Many people are afraid to visit buildings which, over the years, have become associated with the mythology of the occult. Interest in this area has become so diverse that scientists have created a new branch of scientific study: parapsychology.

What has aroused such a sustained interest in psychic phenomena? Nothing seems so appealing to people than the chance of gaining a glimpse of their own destiny, of the future. It is this interest in the future that compels many persons to look for a key either in the occult or through the sixth sense. Others are motivated by a curiosity about their ancestors. All of us are deeply concerned about the present, which proves so difficult to grasp because of its ever-accelerating rate of change; for our brain, the marvelous instrument that it is, transforms everything into the past as soon as it happens.

Another reason for the interest in these phenomena is the discovery of the occult powers of the mind which can be developed, with constant effort, to insure success in life. The human mind has within itself an enormous amount of energy which lies dormant. Many of history's vital personalities discovered and utilized this dormant energy for their own ends; others used it for the benefit of mankind. People who do not make any effort to enlarge and effectively use this potential energy pass through life without experiencing anything beyond the backyard of the small world which has become their precinct.

The area which studies such questions is referred to as practical psychology. In recent years publishers have sent forth many best-sellers on the subject of enlarging the powers of the mind, and one speculates just how many more books on the subject can be absorbed by an ever-hungry public.

Within the sixth sense exists another function, mainly concerned with the appraisal of beauty. This view is not generally accepted despite the fact that the aesthetic sense is considered an addition to the five senses. At the academic level the study of beauty is pursued in the department of philosophy rather than as a pure science. However, in order to inject a balanced perspective into the aesthetic sense, it should be viewed from both scientific and philosophical levels.

This may be an opportune time to focus on a conflict thus far without solution: on the one hand, we have the men of science with their dogmatic attitude trying to explain the spiritual phenomena of life through mathematics, genetics, and electrons; on the other hand, we have the philosopher and theologian, who cast aspersions on the changeable and often fallible role of science. And there seems little basis for reconciliation.

It is then imperative to merge these two seemingly diverse points of view as each approach, in its own context, is correct. The day is approaching when we will be able to discover the link that will couple these diverse theories toward a common end.

In the above paragraphs, we tried to present on a limited scale an idea through which the anatomy and physiology of our sixth sense will be better understood. When putting forward such a theory, each investigator to date has concocted and used a different terminology—more often than not creating a jargon of new phraseology—and thus giving a wide latitude for controversy.* Although each new theory is presented with conviction and sincerity, it is countered by a handful of others disproving it. While it is not easy to brand a theory as erroneous, its validity must stand on an adequate interpretation of the facts.

Sixth-sense manipulations are brain functions, according to Semon's terminology, and considered engrammes. As a consequence, Semon claims that they should be the subject of an anatomical and physiological study. An engramme, according to the *New Standard Dictionary* (1938) is "a tendency which is supposedly imparted to the nucleus undergoing variations and which is inherited by transference of the nuclei to the germ cells." However, according to a definition in a recent dictionary we find the engramme defined as "a persistent protoplasmic change hypothesized to occur on stimulations of living neural tissue and to account for memory." Maybe the truth of the matter is to be found in a combination of these two definitions. I feel it necessary and more reasonable to say that outside forces create a mental footprint which is incorporated through our nervous system into the brain (e.g., the first time a child experiences heat), and that each brain reacts differently in accordance with a unique plan of organization in the individual; there is a corresponding engramme for each stimulus, but it will vary depending on the stimulus and the individual response to it.

## MODERN COGNITIVE PSYCHOLOGY

This is the reason why the phrase "external world" varies in meaning in accordance with the external focusing context in which the observer places himself. Each new experience modifies the internal structure of the particular individual, even though the immediate action rapidly recedes. Each experience leaves an engraphic footprint on the brain, where it will remain indefinitely. This explains why the conduct of a person during a given moment

---

***Babelism in language; see *Babelism,* J. M. Sanchez-Perez, Exposition Press.**

is not only conditioned by external factors, but is also shaped by those experiences already engraved in his brain.

Consequently, when we try to predict an individual's reaction to a given situation, indigenous factors intervene, and this knowledge is very difficult to obtain even when studying ourselves. Each brain assumes a change following an event. Its reaction invariably differs from one time to the next even though the external factors may be consistent. At the present Semon's terminology is not as widely used, but reputable neurologists like Prof. J. M. Nielson, do apply psychiatry through the study of engrammes.

Again people persist in sidelighting the subject with new names. J. C. Young refers to engrammes as "models." In my book *Babelism* I have analyzed how people change names in numerous areas of science in order to enhance their own position. Why confuse the public by introducing alternatives to already adequate terminology?

## THE SIXTH SENSE AS THE AESTHETIC SENSE

Beauty is not a quality of any object, according to the Spanish philosopher and surgeon Novoa Santos, and this is why it lacks an objective reality. Since beauty is not an inherent quality of any object, it appears to us as the expression of a special relationship between the beholder and the object. Even when the object is the product of the beholder's fantasy, this can be categorized as subjective theory in the aesthetic field.

Each of us is capable of distinguishing between the pleasant and the unpleasant. Plato tells us first about the two senses used in the perception of beauty: the eye and the ear. But Vischer was the first to refer to these two faculties as the "aesthetic senses." "An object is beautiful," says Novoa Santos, "or seems to us beautiful when we feel it beautiful. However, this internal sense that permits us to appreciate the internal beauty is neither acoustic, optic, nor associated with any of the five senses." The eye and ear are merely sensorial instruments which help awaken within us the internal feeling of beauty. The subtle feeling that we reecive when we touch a work of art is what Lipps refers to as "a mysterious organ of our inner life," which is a prophetic introduction to my theory, which follows later in this book. It seems there is an external source of beauty which appears to originate outside, but it is the aesthetic qualities from our own thoughts that are transformed into fantastic images.

The aesthetic quality can be found in two areas of the brain: the creation of beauty with a hypothalamic component, and the faculty for the judgment of beauty in the frontal lobe. This is why man can adopt two positions as a critic: as self-critic when he judges his interior thought, and exocritic when he passes judgment on the aesthetic quality of a work of art. The same sixth sense of Du Bois is employed in these two aspects of the spiritual instrument which analyzes beauty. In my opinion it employs this same sixth sense using different "bundles" of engrammes.

According to Novoa Santos, modern art cannot qualify as being beautiful. Santos says, "From the possible lines and figures some hit us more sympathetically than others." I don't think that we can entirely condone his view, when each of the aesthetic pleasures or impressions produced in us results from various forms and figures developed from geometric figures. For if cubism is pure geometry and color, what can we say of modern art? Each of the aesthetic impressions received produces in us forms and figures developed from geometric principles.

Examining modern art, one gets the impression that the practice is an intellectual optic abrasion complex. Sensorial errors and poor judgment can be compared to what one sees when looking through a combination of lenses, prisms, and angular and curved mirrors. Modern artists expect us to believe that they perceive their images in this fashion. Undoubtedly, these are not sensorial abrasions, but some kind of intellectual wearing which allows them to decompose and compose an object in the image plane at will.

Returning to the Santos concept of beauty, the real aesthetic value is based on its biological utility. He mentions the Freudian pansexualism concept that was prominent in his day and considers that it could be confused with the aesthetic pleasures. In order to independent of the observer. He established the two extremes: the beautiful and the horrific, the elegant and the coarse, the tragic and the sublime. But in Plato there always coexisted the moralist and the politician with the aesthetic personality. He questioned Homer for the lack of majestic presence in his descriptions. He also thought that the world was more in need of laws than poetry. This is why Plato initiated the arts of sociology and pedagogy. But in the aesthetic context, it seems to me that his most important concept was the existence of beauty itself as something independent of man but acceding to the fact that some men may be truly able to appreciate beauty.

# 2

# SUGGESTION, HYPNOSIS, AND THE FOURTH DIMENSION

## SUGGESTION

It is important to define the scientific meaning of suggestion, differentiating it from a subtle order or piece of friendly advice and placing it in its proper perspective of persuasion by suggestion. Suggestion is the method or faculty by which one can be influenced by another person, or influence another person. From the classic point of view, suggestion is an external phenomenon that should be differentiated from the normal psychic processes with which it has a lesser degree of similarity. Such processes are hyperacusia, which is an extremely acute sense of hearing, and paralysis, which is the loss of feeling and mobility. However, hyperacusia and paralysis are extraordinary phenomena which can be produced and reproduced by suggestion.

In the same category we find suggestion related to the everyday experiences to which a person is subjected by others. Berheim defines suggestion as "the act by which one idea is introduced and accepted by another brain." This is an erroneous concept for according to it, any teaching—read or discussed—can be called a suggestive mechanism. What we have here is a case of Babelism in language, impeding us from differentiating between the psychological and pathological states.

Generally, in the physiological state, we are at liberty to act according to our wishes and are held responsible for our actions while under suggestion, though when the mind is under hypnosis the subject is apt to lose both the sense of responsibility and free will. Claude Bernard's studies claimed that physiological phenomena are of the same nature as psychological phenomena:

functions are deviated, modified, altered, or abolished. Because of this, hallucinations and delirium are of the same nature as sleep. Suggestion and persuasion, along with the other processes of influence, have similarities; being different by their own characteristics the pathological processes belong to the same "synthesis" but their evolution varies from the psychological point of view.

What are the characteristics of suggestion that differentiate it from an order, discussion, or demonstration? In the case of an order the subject obeys the command, accepting the task, though he may object to it. The spontaneity with which the subject performs the task is the result of an exterior influence. On the contrary, the subject of suggestion obeys without criticism, judgment, or reasoning: he simply obeys. The difference is subtle but significant.

Charcot observed that in the case of certain subjects it is possible to make them accept by suggestion a group of coherent ideas associated with the spirit in such a way that they can produce motor phenomena. Janet keeps this curious metaphor: "Suggestions are truly parasites of the thoughts in their automatic and independent development." I do not agree that this is always true, as many suggestions are favorable to the individual and we could better classify them as symbiotic. Suggestion from a distance or from outer space does not exist, nor can it be demonstrated scientifically.

Suggestion in time does exist and is accepted scientifically, provided it is enacted under hypnotism and a suggestion is given for a precise time. For instance, a person under hypnosis can be told that he will drink a glass of water at a specific time in the future and when he is conscious, and indeed does so.

It is also possible for a person who has been subjected to suggestion many times to develop an association with a certain idea and be able to autosuggest in instances where he meets with a similar idea or image. Should you subject yourself to hypnosis many times in order to learn how to react to a certain difficulty, you shall discover that when you encounter the difficulty in the conscious state your reaction will generally be the one you learned while under hypnosis. Here again the engrammes have an important role. In many cases of traumatic hysteria autosuggestion acts in a very predominant way. This is the reason why hypnosis is being employed in therapy to a greater degree today than at any time in the past.

At various times in our history people have sought hope and inspiration by focusing on a brilliant point; as a result, the masses in question may envelop themselves in a stupor. This is known as fascination. In ordinary times it can be achieved quite easily by asking a subject to look into an expert's eyes who is capable of mesmerizing him in a short time.

The suggestion that we have examined thus far only reaches the psyche of the subject. In the subjective state the ego is not involved. This is verified in so-called dual (split) personality cases, such as Dr. Jekyll and Mr. Hyde. From a medical standpoint, each person possesses only one personality, and should a second one emerge it may be considered a sign of mutual disorder.

It may be necessary to separate the functions for deductive reasons, but we must appreciate that the nervous system for the conscious and unconscious functions is under the same system. No function eludes the control of the brain. This is the primary reason why no organ of the body is excluded from suggestion.

## HYPNOSIS

One question which is often asked is: Is everyone capable of being hypnotized? The answer and the statistics vary according to the hypnotist, and there seems to be little agreement on the issue. The reality is that not everyone is receptive to hypnosis. Generally speaking, it can be said that women are better subjects than men, whereas younger people are more receptive than are older persons. Furthermore, people who have been hypnotized a number of times become more favorably disposed to the procedure. It has also been found that people who have observed or assisted at such sessions are better subjects for the hypnotist.

It appears that there is a process of education for the hypnotic subject. At this point it is opportune to state that according to Mesmer's theory on the application of "vital energy," the more you magnetize a certain individual the more his resistance increases toward the magnetizer's influence.

This theory should be kept in mind in order to grasp the differences between hypnotism and magnetism. In reality, nothing permits us to ascertain with certainty the ability to hypnotize a certain person; there are any number of variables, not the least of which is the relationship between the hypnotist and the subject. If one requires factual answers it is best for one to practice the phenomenon and observe.

Curiously, it is at the base of the fingernails that we have sensitive vascular cells. It can be generally affirmed that the desires of a person are of the glomic type, and it is these desires, or at least his willingness, that are necessary in order for the subject to be hypnotized. It is difficult to obtain a satisfactory result when the subject is unwilling. Norzet tells us that it has been known for a long period that one can transform natural sleep into a hypnotic state. The procedure is quite simple: one simply places the index finger slightly above the nose of a subject who has been sleeping for two hours. The hypnotist should adapt the breathing rhythm of the subject a minute or so before touching the subject and maintain the same pace as the subject throughout the procedure. You can then proceed to ask the subject questions and receive coherent answers without the person awakening. The subject can also be asked to simulate the appearance of being in a somnambulistic state.

Once again, the fingers play a very important role in this process. At the base of the fingernails up to four hundred neurovascular elements can be found.

Some experts think that all forms of hypnotism are similar. According to Berheim, hypnotism is a matter of suggestion. I consider this too absolute to be true. It is essential to determine the degree of sensitivity or susceptibility of the subject as well as the ability to create energy on the part of the hypnotist. Berheim also claims that nobody can be hypnotized against his will. While this is generally true there are exceptions. There are people with hypersensitive zones which, when depressed, allow a subject to be hypnotized. This is illustrated by an incident involving a patient of Dr. Pitres. The patient, who was treated and discharged, had hypersensitive zones in her arms. A stranger who touched her arm was able to hypnotize her to a point where he was able to seduce her.

The best known, although not the most fortunate of hypnosis classifications, was given by Charcot and in its day created the basis for what was then called the great hypnotism. In those days hypnosis was presented in three forms: catalepsy, lethargy, and somnambulism.

According to Charcot, the subject in a cataleptic state adopts a posture with his eyes open, a fixed stare, a peculiar placidity, there is no reflex action, complete analgesia is present, and neuromuscular hyperexcitability is nonexistent. Such a subject can see and hear and the muscular senses remain conscious. Through oral command it is possible to produce hallucinations and animations. In this case the subject can be placed in a horizontal position with his body stretched between two chairs (his head on one chair and his feet on the other), and, in this position, a person can stand on the subject's stomach without injuring him.

In the lethargic state the subject appears to be in a deep sleep accompanied by anesthesia in the skin and mucous. The eyes are closed, although a slight flicker can be detected, and the reflexes are increased with a neuromuscular hyperexcitability. When the subject passes into the lethargic state a snoring noise is heard, and occasionally foam forms on the lips of the subject.

The subject in the somnambulistic state appears to be asleep. Rigidity is less accentuated than in the lethargic state. Muscular hyperexcitability may provoke reactions at the slightest contact with the skin. Of course, there is complete absence of pain. Vision, hearing, and smell become heightened, and orders will be executed automatically.

Charcot realized that it was important to study not only all that was related to hypnotism but also to look for somatic changes in order to differentiate truth from fiction and thus convince scientists and skeptics. However, when one studies large groups of hypnotized persons the Charcot concept proves to be inadequate as there are many more variations than those to which he subscribes. Either the three stages do not appear at all, or in the cases where they do appear they are seen in various aspects and intensities. Hypnotism can exist without fixed somatic differentiations. Charcot's classifications may have sufficed in their time, but now hypnosis has been divided into many different parts. Consequently, a broader concept than that envisaged by Charcot must be adopted in order to understand the phenomenon.

From my point of view, the most important functions of hypnosis are in the experimental field and its use in the investigation of the field of the unknown, the communication with spirits, and all other exercises in which a person in a hypnotic state develops more receptivity in the field of perception. The different levels of hypnotic states are the result of the influence of the hypnotist's psi force acting on the subject's brain circulatory process, as observed in my angiograms.

## SPIRITUALISM

In the United States in 1848 John Fox of New York provided an opportunity to investigate the spiritual dimension. Fox, together with his wife and two daughters, began hearing unexplainable noises in their home. The noises, which began as indistinct sounds, changed to a loud knocking rhythm at night. Instead of fearing the noise, the youngest daughter, Katie, age eight, began talking to the source. When Katie requested that "it" change the rhythm of the knocking it acknowledged by doing so.

A startled Mrs. Fox brought the episode a step further when she successfully communicated verbally with the "source." She discovered that it was the spirit of an individual who was murdered in the same house a few years previously. In successive days the spirit told the Fox family that the remains of his mortal body were buried in the basement of the house.

The Old Testament tells us that in 1060 B.C. Saul, forsaken by God for his persecution of psychic and gifted people, visited a witch at Endor. Using the witch as a medium Saul contacted his dead brother Samuel. The witch suspected Saul's intention and cried, ". . . with a loud voice: and the woman spoke to Saul, saying: Why hast thou deceived me? For thou art Saul." Samuel told Saul that the Israelis would be placed at the mercy of the Philistines who would later exterminate them. And, as we know, this came to pass.

I do not believe or disbelieve these two examples. However, bcause of my theory, I am more disposed toward believing such cases.

In a study of how the hypnotized person behaves, Grasset says that the medium transforms himself into a person similar to the subject under hypnosis. In that case Grasset concedes the existence of a dual personality even if it is transitory.

From the French journal *Spirit* we take a case written by Grasset, witnessed by Janet and performed by a medium named D'Alezy. After an ordinary period of somnambulism during which the medium spoke in her own voice, she abruptly changed her pose. Grasset claims that the medium was possessed by a spirit, that of Eliane, a very young girl with theatrical tendencies and a frivolous character. She had to be handled with great caution. "A new change occurs," says Grasset, "now the medium is Gustavo, and we asked him to paint as he claimed to be an artist in real life. He takes time to draw the image of a dog." Grasset records him as saying, "I tried many times to contact you but for that it is necessary to have fluids . . . to communicate with comrades on earth is very difficult, in the unknown we are like birds . . . if I come back to the world I want to be an artist. I will go to school and amuse myself with the models." After this tiring session Miss D'Alezy awoke.

The Grasset comments are slightly sarcastic and bear the tone of a nonbeliever as he was sure he possessed a scientific explanation for the unknown and the supernatural. We could ask Grasset who it was that put the witch at Endor under hypnosis. Maybe Saul himself. We could ask Grasset if it was not Saul himself who telepathically communicated with the witch as he was then in a terrified state and was reputed to be highly sensitive.

You may think there is a discrepancy in what we have just

stated and what was stated previously. First it was said that spiritualism could be supernatural in origin. Now this is contradicted by Grasset's opinion that spiritualism could be conceived in a strictly scientific fashion.

If the mind of the scientist is broad enough to be willing to give credit to something that has not been scientifically verified, and if the spiritualist's mind would cease in its constantly apathetic view of science, then faith and science may just understand each other. They could go a long way toward complementing each other. This could create a harmony that would benefit mankind in his quest for a more balanced understanding of the unknown.

Marie Bell, a contemporary French comedienne, tells us that one day she met an old family friend with whom she had lost contact for some time. Like herself, her friend was a believer in the immortality of the soul. When her friend asked, "Do you have the courage to directly communicate with your father?" Miss Bell was excited by the prospect as she was very attached to her father, who had died several years previously. Miss Bell's friend promised to take her to Rue Copernic in Paris where friends of his were holding a spiritualist meeting.

"I was introduced to these people," she recalls. "In all there were eight persons in this semidark room. In one corner a single lamp burned on a table. We were all very affected by the high level of emotion. The lady of the house asked us to concentrate as everybody present will hear my father's voice. The lady commanded, 'Don't move. Breathe slowly. Above all, don't talk. Absolute immobility.'

"After five minutes of silence the man of the house told me to ask my father a question. My hands grew cold and my legs were trembling. 'Miss Bell, what do you want to ask your father?' Suddenly, I heard my own voice asking, 'Papa, are you happy?' My father answered, 'Yes.' The lady of the house asked the other participants if they had heard the voice; all of them had.

"I was told to ask another question. After a pause I asked, 'Do you participate in my existence? How are you visiting me at home?' He answered, 'The dead never abandon their beloved living. Every night when you go to bed I am there nearby you.' "

Bear in mind the circumstances under which this meeting took place. Miss Bell had been emotionally attached to her father and was in an excited state. An atmosphere of suspense existed as the man of the house sat in front of her staring into her eyes. It is easy to believe that Miss Bell received a suggestion (was receptive) from the man at Rue Copernic while the remainder of the audience were his collaborators. The second possibility is that the lady of the house was a medium previously hypnotized and trained by her husband, and, as in the Grasset case, she received telepathic messages from the spirit of Marie Bell. In the first possibility fraud was the motive. The second case is clearly an example of psychic phenomena.

There is no doubt that in the broad expanse of spiritualism there is much fraud and make-believe. We must also concede that there are genuine cases where for a certain length of time a phenomenon has been sustained, reaching an almost religious level, and maintaining a diversity of sects. But if only one percent of truth exists, we cannot totally discount spiritualism.

Let me give you another instance of plausible spiritualism. Mr. Davis, a famous American medium, speaking in one of his sessions, said, "The spirits do not exist in sessions, but they send their messages from the unknown." He also said, "The spirit is very intangible but measurable."

In the United States in 1855 there were more than two million people involved in various kinds of spiritualism, and today's figure probably exceeds that many times.

## THE FOURTH DIMENSION

Astral projection, or bilocation, is another aspect of psychic phenomena which upsets our conventional concept of a three-dimensional world and our preconceived ideas of the space-time phenomenon.

At the Royal Society of Medicine in 1927 Sir Auckland Geddes told of an out-of-the-body experience he had at a time when he was quite ill. The incident involved his being in two places at the same time. Sir Auckland says, "I was free in a time dimension of space, where 'now' was in some way equivalent to 'here' in the ordinary three-dimensional space of everyday life."

In 1870, at Leipzig, Frederick Zollner, a professor of physics, tried to prove the existence of a fourth dimension by studying certain occult phenomena. He was aware that objects could appear and disappear without physical explanation. Zollner, using a medium, asked her to make a knot in a plain loop of wire. The medium succeeded in tying three knots in the loop without touching the wire. Zollner concluded that some kind of force (spiritual or otherwise) was involved; at present the phenomenon of bending metal has been studied by Prof. J. Hasted, who described the internal dynamic strain in the paranormal bending of metal in March 1978 at Trinity College.

In 1882 the Society of Psychical Research was founded. Its purpose was to study mesmeric phenomena, hypnosis and its aspects, and the like. Prof. Henry Siegwick was its first president.

Lawrence Cook was a famous medium who lived in London in 1870 and who saw strange forms which became known as ectoplasm. Cook was the subject of an interesting study by Dr. William Crookes, who discovered thallium and the fluorescent lamp.

Ectoplasm is a white fluid substance whose origin is thought to be in the mouth of the medium and is sometimes emitted through the pores of the skin. This mysterious substance, which has never been examined in a laboratory, can be photographed (according to Richet) and has the appearance of filaments. Other investigators claim to have touched it. Sir Arthur Conan Doyle is said to have had such an experience in a session with a medium called Eve C. (Marth Beraud, born in Algiers, 1905). Sir Arthur said he had felt the ectoplasm as if it were a live substance.

It has also been observed that if mediums are weighed before and after the emission of ectoplasm, some lose up to six pounds. Such weight could be consumed in the creation of ectoplasm. At the International Conference of Parapsycologists in Mexico

City (1974), Dr. Robert Tocquet presented a paper entitled, "Psychical Phenomena." In it he showed the materialization of psychic energy (ectoplasm), which formed hands and feet, using the paraffin technique. The method involves placing paraffin in a receptacle and leaving it in the area where the ectoplasm is expected to form. In three instances the paraffin was controlled by the addition of cholesterol.

Similar cases of this nature were recorded in Warsaw, Poland, where they also employed the paraffin technique but did not use cholesterol. While Dr. Tocquet's paper only quotes the Warsaw instances in passing, he guarantees the Paris findings as these experiments were conducted under his supervision.

Epes Sargent, in his book *The Scientific Basis of Spiritualism* tells us, "On an occasion one of the assistants at a session took a knife from his pocket and tried to cut one of the hands of the ectoplasmic form [of materialized energy]." In this case the medium felt a strong pain as though the knife had actually cut her hand. The assistant felt very happy as he was convinced that he had uncovered the fraudulent nature of the session and hoped to see the medium's hand cut. Although the medium's hand was not cut or scratched, she experienced a pain and cutting sensation several hours later. If this incident is true, we must increase research and seek an explanation.

"The production of ectoplasm gives opportunity," according to Louis Spense, "for materialization, which is the temporal physical manifestation of the spirit, which can only be seen but which itself can touch people." Hands and feet are the most frequent forms which materialize; arms and legs are less common. Only in rare instances does the entire body materialize in ectoplasmic form. Occasionally, the materialization can also take the form of an animal. Using this as a theme, Sir Arthur Conan Doyle wrote the story, "Playing with Fire," and although it may be a work of fiction the story is plausible. Dr. Tocquet also assures us that in one session he touched and petted the manifested form of a dog.

Materialization generally begins with the formation of a whitish mass wherever the session is taking place. Generally, it keeps "growing" until it takes the form of a hand or leg. It is possible to touch it, and, if the form is that of a person, it may talk.

A well-known medium, Eusapia Palladino, became famous for her ability to produce ectoplasm. She was probably the first most complete medium to become the subject of intensive and prolonged scientific investigation in a half-dozen countries.

Born in the remote Italian village of Minervino Murge, near Bari, Eusapia was orphaned early in her life (her mother died at the time of her birth and her father was murdered a few years later). She was unable to attend school and had to work in the village fields.

She attracted attention because she was able to produce strange phenomena with great frequency. These included rapping sounds, noises of various kinds, and the movement of objects. Her peculiar powers were brought to the attention of a Mr. Damiani, who had an interest in the occult. He took the girl, then twenty years old, to Naples where she met Dr. Ercole Chinia, who diagnosed hysteria as the root of her strange actions.

In 1891 Dr. Chinia invited the world-famous Italian psychiatrist Cesare Lombroso to examine Eusapia. Accompanied by other scientists, Lombroso subjected the girl to stringent tests by making her move furniture, produce ectoplasm, and initiate noises and rapping. The examination was conducted under such controlled conditions that the venerable body of scientists, along with Lombroso, were convinced of the girl's authenticity. This gave Eusapia the opportunity to organize seances in Milan, where people of the stature of Nobel prize winner (in medicine) Charles Richet, the astronomer Schiaparelli, and the German philosopher Karl Freiherr du Prel were impressed by the genuine nature of her achievements, all of which were practiced in daylight in contrast to the subdued and dimly lit sessions of the spiritualist.

The flocking of such eminent men of science to see Eusapia brought the girl to the attention of Europe. In 1893 she was invited by Prof. Julius Ochorwicz to visit Warsaw. Using electric controls and a dynamometer, he was able to prove that while Eusapia was experiencing psychical activity, his assistants were losing their psychical force. (In the last chapter of this book my organic theory will offer a feasible explanation for these phenomena.)

Dr. Charles Richet invited Eusapia to France where Sir Oliver Lodge, Dr. Myers, Prof. Siegwick, and Dr. Schrench-Notring from Munich examined her. They witnessed her being able to make a piano play while her fingers were eighteen inches away from the keyboard. The results were so astounding that many scientists wanted to repeat the tests in England. Then Eusapia was invited to Cambridge where she demonstrated her abilities to many academicians and scientists. Although they could not determine the source of her strange powers, they viewed her feats with skepticism. Being herself intrigued, she suggested that she should be placed on a scale. While standing on the scale she levitated a table which was positioned at the far end of the room. The scale indicator registered the weight of the table as being added to her own weight while the table remained levitated.

The scientific community concluded that Eusapia Palladino was able to produce some kind of energy responsible for her accomplishments and the levitation of the table.

One question that arose from the observation of her actions was the possibility of her being aided by a spirit. It was thought that if it could be proved that Eusapia was aided by a spirit, it would give validity to the theory that life goes on after death.

The scientific attention devoted to Eusapia Palladino generated an unprecedented interest and flow of knowledge in this area. This knowledge awoke the latent potential of many great mediums.

As a scientist I fully appreciate the fact that there are many fraudulent individuals and groups involved in this field. Science should only investigate that small group of mediums who are proved genuine. Their achievements should be scrutinized with care, and investigators should keep in mind that a medium's mystic powers are not always at the disposal of the individual.

In relation to parapsychological phenomena, Franz Anton Mesmer and Wilhelm Reich devoted much time to the study of the fact that the human being could only communicate with the exterior through the known five senses. It is ironic that for years Mesmer was considered the father of hypnosis. His hypnotic procedures were utilized for some time and came to be known as mesmerism. What Mesmer actually achieved was a way to cure some diseases.

Reich was the founder of orgonomy, which he defines as cosmovital energy. According to him this energy appears as an aura around humans and animals. After carefully studying Mesmerism, Reich concluded that the aura was responsible for magnetic phenomena as well as hypnosis, and that it affected also its alterations when the subject perception of an objective energy interferes with the magnetic aura. According to his study, subjective perceptions are directed to the center where they produce anxiety.

Reich claimed, "The cosmovital energy reaches the subject in a variety of forms. In the case of dowsing, the medium uses wires, rods, or branches, but there are some mediums who do not require the help of these instruments in order to detect the existence of water, minerals, or petroleum." They have enough concentrated cosmovital energy to put themselves in a receptive state to find minerals.

If this could be proved we could conclude that thoughts are tangible as they are attracted to substance. If this is studied in the light of my theory, it could be compared with the phenomenon known as psychometry. Reich said, "Mesmer discovered the universal fluid which is capable of penetrating all matter." We are aware of the fact that Mesmer's critics denied the existence of that fluid, but now, more than two hundred years later, the existence of certain energies emerging from the body have been verified. Many of Mesmer's patients described a bluish gray aura emerging from his fingers. The fingers are used in order to sense many things, and I shall use this later in the book to support my organic theory. It was in 1944 that Reich demonstrated, by means of X rays, the existence of orgonomic energy between the palms of the hands. However, the interpretation of the X rays is open to discussion and further analysis.

# 3

# THE SIXTH SENSE IN THE PERCEPTION OF THE OCCULT

In recent times much interest in the occult has been generated in the United States, along with the Soviet Union and its satellites. Research is constantly being done in the Soviet city of Akadengorod in an effort to put the subject into perspective.

Much has been written about phenomena such as vision without eyesight and other unnatural body powers. I am reminded of what Christine Garnier, the French writer, said about a friend "living in Paris in a complete state of poverty, restricting her possessions to a crucifix, a bed, a table, a spoon, and a fork. This person lives in complete poverty, living among the invisible and in the sixth sense." Doctors have examined the woman and verified some of her strange powers. For example, she can focus on a television antenna and describe exactly the content of the programs being received.

"I don't know the reason for the phenomena," continues writer Garnier, "but I trust my friend of twenty years and I believe what she tells me about the future." Garnier thinks her medium friend undoubtedly possesses psychic abilities and great mental power. Self-imposed poverty must contribute to the development of her powers. It is well known that the less a person is attached to material things the higher the mind and the soul elevate themselves, giving us the opportunity to observe the sixth sense and its perception of the occult.

It was Dr. Charles Reich, who in the later part of the last century, proposed the name "parapsychology" to designate phenomena that go beyond the known senses. Some people term such extraordinary powers as part of "the sixth sense." At the Utrecht Congress early this century, the Germans proposed calling the study of such phenomena "metapsychics." Today, such phenomena are confusingly referred to by the three names.

From these observations we can conclude that these phenomena are now being subjected to serious study in a dozen countries. Furthermore, we know too that all people possess such powers in varying degrees although most people rarely use them. Most people go through life without exploring their psychic potential. What does vary from person to person is the organic constitution of the individual.

One of the most intriguing studies in the area of parapsychology is the ability of some persons to see without using their eyes. This is known as extraocular vision. This name was given to Alan Ames from the United States and Rosa Kulskova from Ursk in the Soviet Union because of their ability to see without using their eyes and being able to distinguish colors by touch.

Many cases of this kind have been noted, but we will confine ourselves to the most interesting. The Russian girl was born into a family suffering from congenital blindness. Although not blind herself, she learned the Braille method of reading. While learning Braille she learned that she could also see with the tips of her fingers. She was subjected to examination at the Moscow Neurological Institute, where doctors established that her ability was genuine. The doctors and scientists also concluded that the girl did not identify objects simply by means of touch, but that she did see with the tips of her fingers. When photographs were presented to the girl she could quickly identify persons and objects. What is more amazing is that she could also perform the same actions with her feet.

Cesare Lombroso tells of a hysterical patient who lost his eyesight and gradually began acquiring the facility to see with the tip of his nose and his earlobes. In another case, Margaret Foos, a fourteen-year-old American girl, could see perfectly when blindfolded. Ved Metha, an Indian girl, lost her sight when she was three years old. By the time the girl reached adolescence she was able to cycle through the streets and, according to her statement, could "see through the skin of the face." These occurrences are far more common than realized.

## REINCARNATION AND EXTRACEREBRAL MEMORY

These two phenomena are also included within the realm of parapsychology. These unusual happenings revolve around the fundamental idea that after the body dies, the spirit migrates to another body or momentarily transfers from one body to that of an animal. Since 1956 Jashar University in Jaipur, India, has been examining these phenomena with a scientific criterion divorced from either the Hindu religion or occultism. In a meeting with philosopher Daya Krishna, historian G. C. Panday, mathematician G. C. Patri, sociologist T. K. N. Unnithan, and psychologist H. N. Banarjee, they decided to change the name of "reincarnation" to "extracerebral memory." They considered that this term was more in agreement with modern psychology.

Reincarnation and extracerebral memory may be explained as the result of a reception phenomenon. Last year, on our visit to Jaipur, we tried to meet Prof. Banarjee, but he was on vacation.

According to Banarjee this term is adequate for scientific research as reincarnation could also involve spiritualism and occultism and therefore confuse the issue. The group of scientists considered it necessary to study individual cases in the environment in which they occurred. To date the group has studied over eighty cases involving instances of extracerebral memory. Since 1962 the group has been aided by Prof. Ian Stevenson of the Department of Neurology and Psychiatry at the University of Virginia. They have successfully tested people as far away as Turkey, where reincarnation is contrary to the belief of Muslims.

It was in Bahçe, Turkey, that the group observed one of the most intriguing cases since they began their study. A farmer named Suzulmus and one of his wives and two of his three sons were found murdered. A few months later in a nearby village a butcher's wife gave birth to a boy. They named their ninth child Ismail. He was born with a visible depression in his cranium. The scar-like depression disappeared when Ismail was two years old. When the boy was only three years old he told the family that he did not want to live with them as his real name was Suzulmus. He said he wished to return to his old house to live with his only living son. After questioning he revealed the details of the murder. The boy was so persevering that his father finally took him to the Bahçe house where he not only recognized the farm but also many of his neighbors and even some customers who he claimed owed him money at the time of his death. All these events could hardly have been imported into the mind of a three-year-old boy.

The daughter of André Maurois, Michelle, is convinced that she has lived on earth before and tells of her encounter with a woman whom she knew in her past life. The woman Michelle met asked if she had visited Australia. Michelle had not. She then asked if Michelle had lived in the Middle Ages. Michelle claimed that she had lived in a castle in the Pyrenees. Both women went to visit the castle and without searching they found an unknown secret passage and revealed much about the ruins which were then unknown to present-day historians.

The women then separated and Michelle conducted telepathic conversations with her friend for many years. She was telepathically informed of the circumstances surrounding her friend's death.

## UBIQUITY

The phenomenon whereby one is seen in two places at the same time is known as "ubiquity." The same is so when a person sees himself in another place. It is frequently found among artists, inventors, and persons with a vivid imagination. The story is told that Catherine of Russia ordered her guards to shoot at her double, which appeared at regular intervals in various parts of her palace. Elizabeth I of England saw herself mortally ill some weeks before she, in fact, fell ill and died. This was not just a premonition but ubiquity, as she claims to have actually seen herself.

Christianity accepts the possibility of ubiquity in cases such as Saint Anthony of Padua. In 1226 Saint Anthony was seen on Holy Thursday preaching a sermon in Limoges Cathedral and simultaneously at a small convent on the outskirts of the city. The Church also admits that Saints Ambrose, Clement, and Severus were in possession of such a gift. Saint Alfonsus Liguori, who was in jail in Arezzo, was seen comforting Clement XIV, who was on his deathbed at the Vatican.

It seems that in certain given parapsychic conditions the psychic part can leave the material part of the body but can still remember both experiences. In 1929 Sylvan J. Muldoon, in collaboration with Hereward Carrington, published a book entitled *Projection of the Astral Body,* which consisted of the memoirs of Muldoon on the subject of ubiquity. Later, Englishman Oliver Fox claimed he was also capable of leaving his body and presented his experiences in a book entitled *Astral Projection.*

Recently, a number of papers have appeared on the subject. In 1960 Dr. Robert Crookall did a study documenting over three hundred different examples of ubiquity and its variants. Six years later, Dr. Charles T. Tart initiated a research program of ubiquity tests which he has continued at the University of California at Davis. In 1971, Dr. Karlis Osis, Director of the American Society of Parapsychologists, also began research in this area.

## PSYCHOMETRY

As I have mentioned in my book *Babelism,* the word "psychometry" has many different meanings. The most common explanation of psychometry states that by means of an intermediary object a sensitive person may obtain paranormal information. Such a person may be able to reveal the history of an object and of events related to its owner. Experts believe that the object used serves as a conductor. Some say such a person is clairvoyant. Still a third group refers to automatic writing as psychometry.

Automatic writing—writing while in a nonconscious state—

is sometimes referred to as psychic writing. It is considered as a psychoautomatism which can also present itself in the forms of talking and thinking.

In 1907 the British archaeologist Blight-Bond and his colleague Captain Bartlett were experimenting with automatic writing. In one instance Bartlett was holding a pencil while talking to Blight-Bond when suddenly the latter asked, "And what about Glastonbury Abbey?" After a pause the pen in Bartlett's hand began writing, "All knowledge is eternal and should be met with mental empathy."

Both men were intrigued when they read the answer and began asking more questions. The pencil wrote the answers in classical Latin saying that the chapel was built by a Father Beere in honor of Edward the Martyr and later remodeled by Father Whiting, who was the last prior of Glastonbury. Following this the pencil drew a map describing an entrance located five feet behind the altar and a chapel extending thirty feet east with horizontal windows in stone and blue-stained glass. The mysterious entity responsible for the motion of the pen revealed that his name was Gughelmus Monacus (William the Monk). With this information the two men discovered the ruins of the chapel.

In another session and using English of the sixteenth century Blight-Bond and Bartlett received instructions to dig in the north part of the abbey. They proceeded to do so and discovered much of what was revealed by William the Monk.

During the following years Blight-Bond and Bartlett accumulated hundreds of messages about the same abbey, the authenticity of which were confirmed by its excavators. Once again they asked who was giving the information. This time the answer came from two monks, both of whom were living at the abbey at different times. On certain occasions the pencil paused for periods revealing that the gaps were caused by discussions between the two monks. One of the informers said his name was Johannes Brant, who died in 1533. Again the archeologists digging at the site found the information to be precise, but discarded the notion that the information could have been automatically written by Bartlett.

## POLTERGEISTS

"Poltergeist" is a German term designating the paranormal phenomenon of a psychic nature such as unexplained noises, the floating of objects in the air, or the unexplained falling of objects from elevated places. Spiritualists attribute all these phenomena to the presence of spirits. However, from a purely psychological standpoint, it has been observed that in most cases an adolescent person must be present for the occurrence of such phenomena.

The German word is derived from *polter* (to make noise) and *geist* (ghost) and literally means noisy ghosts. In the following situation we have an example of telekinesis, "ghosts," and the presence of an adolescent. Norman Blundson observes, "One entity or destructive agent provoking noises, throwing objects at random, destroying domestic utensils . . . this spontaneous phenomenon is ordinarily observed in the presence of an adolescent near the age of puberty. It is as if a young person is being persecuted by a ghost. The presence of another spirit may add further commotion to the phenomenon. The unexplained throwing of small pebbles is another characteristic. These pebbles are observed to be hot on falling to the ground."

In 1882 Cesare Lombroso began documenting the extraordinary events taking place at his house in Pescatori Street in the northern Italian city of Turin. Wash basins began emptying water on occupants, bells began ringing for no apparent reason, the people of the house found themselves being pricked with pins, noises of spirits and shadows began to haunt the place, and objects continued to move around the house at random during this time. All this commotion was observed when one of the Lombroso daughters was present. It is important to note that she was never the victim of any of these freak occurrences and was apparently favored by the spirit.

Two Italian sisters, Alina and Santina, became well known in 1959 for creating pebble showers. Such showers were most intense when the girls were asleep, as if activated by their dreams.

It is also worth noting that the majority of persons involved in such cases are female.

At the International Parapsychology Congress in Mexico City (1974) Dr. William Rool told of a case involving a house in Miami where an elderly couple between sixty and seventy years old resided. Objects began moving without reason. The activity became so intense that the couple had to move to a new location. Once again the disturbance continued to interrupt their lives. Their grandson, Roger, was living with them at this time. Dr. Rool placed the seventeen-year-old boy under his care. The boy worked at a gift shop. Dr. Rool observed many objects in the shop moving about freely.

In regard to the boy, Dr. Rool discovered in his psychological studies that the boy directed an unusual amount of hostility toward his father. After observing the trajectory of the falling objects, Dr. Rool concluded that the objects always traveled in the direction of the boy.

The Hungarian psychologist Nandor Feodor describes the poltergeist as the spirit of a disturbed human being. People with deep and profound complexes, says Feodor, can live after their death, changing themselves into energy nuclei and acting against objects. Whereas Dr. Rool attributes these happenings to young adolescent boys and girls, Dr. Feodor cites examples of young people who have died.

To understand the poltergeist through the application of my theory, these young people create the energy in their brain and direct it through the antenna toward the objects that move by means of an unconscious process. Researchers have noted that these phenomena present themselves with more frequency in times of uncertainty, crisis, and extreme tension.

## PREMONITION AND PRECOGNITION

Initially, it is important to distinguish between the often-confused terms "premonition" and "precognition." Premonition is the phenomenon during which paranormal peception warns us in advance about an unforeseen event. Precognition is paranormal perception of the knowledge of a future event.

Premonition is one of the less-complicated areas of study included in the broad context of parapsychology. All of us have experienced premonitions to some degree or another. We have all had hunches or intuitive feelings which have signaled us in advance about a moment of danger. It is not uncommon to hear people say, "I was afraid that was going to happen." Such a statement does not qualify as a premonition. The information must be stated without any relation to the senses and always written down at the time of its occurrence for future verification.

Louis Pauwels, in his book *Return of the Witches,* describes a scene where he was walking on Rue Gay-Lusac in Paris one afternoon. At about four o'clock he saw black, nondescript masses coming toward him and smaller masses flying around him. He kept walking and people began observing him closely. He did not experience any organic disorder. Pauwels felt that something was wrong with his stepfather, a great mystic and an amicable type of person.

When he returned home he found his stepfather in an emotionally disturbed state. The man recounted that he had been confronted by a very grave spiritual crisis, during the course of which he had been tempted to kill himself. The time of the crisis coincided with the disturbances experienced by Pauwels while walking in Rue Gay-Lusac.

A second experience recounted by Pauwels occurred in the form of a dream. As he neared waking he heard the voice of his eleven-year-old son. Pauwels said, "My son was shouting, 'Father, I am drowning,' but when I awoke I dismissed the incident as a bad dream." Several hours later he received a telephone call from the small town of Trouville, where his son was on vacation. His son, François, had been severely burned by firecrackers which had been ignited in his pocket, and he was in critical condition.

The two events could have been clearly monitored by telepathy and need not necessarily be attributed to a premonition;

I believe the latter to be a complex phenomenon consisting of certain characteristics also common to telepathy and clairvoyance. In general, researchers have found that premonitions occur while dreaming.

The classic example of a premonition is that of a passenger about to board a plane and changing his plans at the last minute because he feels something will happen during the flight. If something happened to the plane, this would be considered a genuine premonition.

Clairvoyance in dreams is not uncommon. Dreams can be both clairvoyant and precognitive. The manner in which trance-like states or sleep bring the subconscious to the conscious is not understood, but in it lies the knowledge and power of the transcendental self.

Let us consider the following example. Mrs. Maria Luongo, who lived in Naples, Italy, awoke in a frightened state on a summer morning in 1953. She had seen an image of her eight-year-old-son, Tancredo, which perplexed her. This startled her as her son was at a Boy Scout camp several miles from Naples. What excited her even more was the appearance of her son: his clothes were torn and he appeared very weak. Mrs. Luongo was convinced that her vision preceded something horrific. She immediately decided to travel to the camp and look for her son. At the campsite she found her son exactly as he had appeared in her vision.

Some investigators might conclude that Mrs. Luongo was afraid that her son was having a bad experience and that she was subconsciously provoking a vision or a hallucination. But I ask myself if the maximum anguish situation in which the boy found himself could not have made him generate enough energy in order to call to his mother for help. If this was the case, it would be a good example of telepathy.

Intuitive feelings or hunches were mentioned at the beginning of this section. They are of great importance in cases where a gifted clairvoyant is connected with a police department or security force. Patrolman Don Sabel of Grosse Pointe Woods, Michigan, solved several cases after directing his investigations along the lines of information received through hunches and other strange sensations.

In the case of another law officer, Inspector John Seeney had fallen asleep in his chair one evening at London's Scotland Yard. Suddenly, an undescribable sensation awakened him and a strong feeling drove him to leave the building. This strange sensation saved his life; only minutes after he left the building a bomb was detonated a few steps from his office.

Again we will look at another case of telepathy that could be interpreted as a premonition. A Wisconsin mother, Mrs. Hoffman, lost her five-year-old son, Max. The night following the burial, Mrs. Hoffman had a dream in which she saw her son awakening in his coffin and trying to free himself. She awoke screaming and begged her husband to take her to the grave. Mr. Hoffman thought it was a nightmare caused by the emotional experience of the tragedy.

The following night Mrs. Hoffman had a similar dream. She saw a vision of her son cringing in his small coffin with an expression of pain on his face. Mr. Hoffman, with a neighbor, went to the cemetery. Working with a lantern the men began to unearth the coffin. Opening the casket they found Max curled up, just as his mother had seen him in her dreams on two successive nights.

He was taken to a local doctor's house. After one hour of resuscitation procedure, Max Hoffman opened his eyes and started breathing. A week later the boy had fully recovered. He lived in Clinton, Iowa, for another eighty years, saving as his most valued possession the handles of the coffin in which he spent two days and nights when a boy.

Fernando Gravey was a famous Belgian actor who recounts a vivid experience during the time he was conscripted as a junior cavalry officer. He was dispatched on a patrol maneuver in the north of Belgium. Along with seven other men he was following a trail outlined on his map. The corporal in the party, who was an uneducated man, told Gravey not to proceed in their present direction. With surprise Gravey asked if the party had lost its way. The corporal answered, "No," saying that he would prefer to take an alternate route. As Gravey himself was not too confident about his interpretation of the map, he ordered his men to take another route. A few minutes later four mortar shells exploded at the point where the troop would have been had they pursued their original route.

Gravey believed that the corporal, although not versed in military matters, felt an irresistible compulsion to ask him to take another route. The corporal later told him that he had no knowledge of what was going to happen but was very frightened. Gravey calls the case "an alarm bell of destiny." This case is of special interest; in this instance the premonitory experience occurred in a conscious state. It also illustrates the force of conviction of the premonition given the caste difference that was part and parcel of military life in those days.

Of course, it is also possible that the corporal convinced Gravey by means of hypnosis. Many experiments have been conducted in the hypnotic state in which the subject is asked to go somewhere and describe what he sees. Very often the reports are astonishingly accurate. Nowadays, police departments throughout the world are using clairvoyant aids in particular cases. Although the results are often positive the information is usually classified.

## TELEPATHY

The communication of thoughts without the participation of any of the five habitual senses is known as "telepathy." F. W. H. Myers created the word in 1833, but the term was less precise than it is today. Now we understand telepathy as a psychic transmission from one individual to another. Much has been written on the subject and many experiments have been closely observed by scientists. In controlled observations, it is not unusual for scientists to monitor in excess of seventy percent correct answers given by participants when questioned simultaneously.

Dr. Walter Prince of Boston, Massachusetts, has supervised telepathic communication experiences at considerable distance and reported his experiences in detail to the American Society of Psychic Research. Prof. Gibe Murray of Oxford had the opportunity in 1931 to convince Dr. Sigmund Freud of his ability to perform telepathic communication. We need to call attention to the possibility of confusing telepathy with premonition. Before an event can be classified as a telepathic phenomenon an interpersonal communication must be recorded, whereas in a premonition the data need not necessarily originate in another brain. Premonition is the knowing of a happening in advance without the intervention of a human and only through the perception of the psyche. This could also be classified as clairvoyance if the event is within the dimension of the future; it is then termed as precognition premonition or prophecy. Should the phenomenon originate in the past the term applied is "retrogression." As you will easily observe, it is much too involved in verbal frivolity. My own theory, which will be detailed in the final chapter, puts the entire mechanism process into perspective.

Some investigators give the name "Psi-Gamma" to the capacity of certain people to know, to feel, or to perceive paranormally without the use of the five senses. This type of perception goes beyond the limits of time and space; that is, it can refer to past or future events, already known or unknown, nearer or farther beyond occult or unknown endeavors, or simply pure ideas that may be in the universe. The physical cyclical mechanism by means of which the brain process takes place still is unknown, but I feel that if this organic theory is proven it may open a large field for demonstrating the enigmas and explaining them. The different ways in which the paranormal reception of the gifted persons manifests itself varies greatly. Someone listens as if someone is talking to him (excluding the well-known auditory hallucinations). Others see in different types of visions (excluding visual hallucinations). Others are able to perform complicated mathematical operations without mistakes. Some are capable of talking in languages that they don't speak. In certain instances of psychometry or visual touch the tips of the fingers are frequently used. In the last method, the procedure of arterioglomic anastomosis is not known.

Dr. Richard Hudson was very skeptical about people who

claimed to be gifted. In 1887 he went from London to the U.S. in order to study Mrs. Leora Paper in Boston. She claimed a voice was telling her that her aunt was still alive. In fact, it was later confirmed by a letter stating the hour and day of her death. A few years later Mrs. Paper became a very famous medium by doing automatic writing about people she did not know, mainly about dead people whom she did not know. Dr. Hudson used all kinds of methods to discover any trickery or fraud, and in these cases he felt it was not person-to-person telepathy but messages received through the spirits who may be living in the other life. In our understanding, what may remain in the universe are the energies created by the living brains when they were alive, and maybe the receptors of today are tuned to that type of energy, receiving from the universal intelligence what may be.

There is a story that became very famous in Frankfurt when Mr. Rochlitz made a trip to Weimar to visit Goethe, his friend. He failed to find him at home, but he entered the house anyway because he was a close friend and in order to change his clothes, which were very wet because of the rain. A maid gave Mr. Rochlitz a gown and slippers; then he sat down in an armchair to wait and he fell asleep. While sleeping he saw Goethe on the way to Belvedere and he got the impression that Goethe told him, "Frederick, my good friend, what are you doing in Weimar, and why are you wearing my gown and slippers?" While Rochlitz was sleeping Goethe was traveling in the company of Mr. Klemm on the way to Belvedere, and while he was completely awake, he saw his friend Rochlitz walking toward him, wearing his gown and slippers and asking him the same question that he heard while he was sleeping, and that Mr. Klemm heard orally coming out of the mouth of Goethe while they were talking.

Before proceeding I want to talk about personal observations that may prove that telepathy can be involuntary and can occur between people who do not know each other and without relation to time and distance and different receptors.

When I first presented at the Roentgen Ray Society Convention in the Palmer House in Chicago the first model of the automatic Seriograph, several members of that society, after examining my device and seeing it working, told me that they themselves have had the same idea.

Of course, their scientific and social position could not leave a doubt in my mind that their statements were true. When I asked them why they did not put their idea into practice their sincere statements were "lack of time," "difficulty in finding someone capable of making it." Another one told me he lost faith in the utility of what the apparatus could be as angiography in those days was a very complicated procedure. Others did not give any answer as to why. On that occasion curiosity took over my mind if some of them could have been telepathizing their idea to me, but after finding out that none of them had the idea prior to 1946, I felt at ease because I had the idea in 1931. Knowing this my conscience became quiet.

I have observed telepathic occurrences at the same time with two or more persons at different distances in space and being themselves unknown to each other. At the International Congress of Parapsychology that took place in Mexico City, Dr. Julius Eisenbud of Denver University in Colorado informed us of the one-dimension dematerialization in psychophotography. We know this procedure has existed since 1840. When several individuals claimed to have obtained psychophotographics, it gave opportunity to a large discussion as it could not be proved false or genuine. In those days they formed societies of photographers who were capable of getting those psychic photographs in which dead people appeared among the living. In 1870 the results in England were more convincing as they were produced under higher control. In 1913 Fukurae, Japanese, wrote a book and the translation into English was widely extended about this subject. In 1934 two English photographers wrote another book about psychophotography but most of the time a medium was necessary in order to obtain positive results. In 1953 Dr. Eisenbud found two young fellows who were practicing hypnosis and psychic photography capable of photographing small treasures and then finding things that were lost.

It is necessary to emphasize that a medium is necessary in

order to take these photographs, my conclusion being that it is precisely the ability of this gifted person to receive, transform, and then transmit the necessary energy sufra or infra luminos necessary to create the image onto the photographic paper that was sent to him telepathically by the observer.

## CLAIRVOYANCE

Clairvoyance is better defined as a process of knowledge of paranormal quality of events past or present, regardless of distance (prophecy refers to the future while recognition involves knowing in the past).

Carl Gustav Jung, the distinguished Swiss psychiatrist, was awakened from a deep sleep on a summer night in 1926. He was first awakened by the noise of what appeared to be quiet but penetrating steps. Shortly after this he began to perceive that they appeared to be getting closer, and he heard noises which he interpreted as laughing and singing. As his home was located in Böllengem, far from the turbulence of the city proper, he failed to find any rational explanation for the disturbance. When he approached the window, he found no one outside.

He drifted back to sleep only again to be awakened by more singing, this time accompanied by an accordion. Approaching the window, he violently opened it in anger. Again no one was present. The hallucination was so persistent that Professor Jung was not satisfied until he had thoroughly investigated the case. After digging through archives for a few weeks he discovered that the current location of his house once served as a meeting place for young Swiss mountaineers in the springtime. It was here that the young men assembled to enlist as mercenaries for the armies of the various and often-warring Italian republics. It was on this patch of ground that the soldiers would bid farewell to their loved ones amid music and wine.

Clairvoyance is in reality the paranormal phenomenon that is the most complicated. Madame Blavatsky was one of the founders of the Theosophical Society, a small religion based on the following principles: (1) to form a nucleus of universal brotherhood of humanity free from all forms of discrimination, (2) to study comparative religion, and (3) to investigate the unexplained laws of nature and the powers latent in man.

A Swedish lady who served as secretary to Madame Blavatsky wrote a book about her employer and her various clairvoyant experiences. The secretary, Constance Wachtmeister, recounts a journey she made with her employer from Enghien to Paris. During the course of the journey Madame Blavatsky suddenly said that she was listening to *The William Tell Overture,* one of her favorite operas. Intrigued by the statement her secretary investigated and later discovered that at the precise time when her employer claims to have heard the opera it was being performed on the Champs Elysees in Paris. She was perplexed by Madame Blavatsky's feat but later discovered that her employer could hear at very long distances.

For her own part Miss Constance was also the subject of other paranormal experiences. Once when packing for a train trip to Italy to visit Madame Gebbard and her employer, she heard a man's voice ordering her to put a certain manuscript in her luggage. The scripts consisted of a selection of Tarot cards and parts of the Cabala. After she arrived in Italy Madame Blavatsky told her, "The master told me that you have a manuscript that I need urgently." The secretary did not immediately recall packing it. However, on being reminded, she found it.

I have to explain that the Master was one of those entities or mahatmas in whom Theosophists believe, or believed—people who lived in this world, and though they have passed away still influence living persons, always in a positive sense, though not always a pleasant one; i.e., they help them to improve their souls and announce to them past or future deeds, but the ones chosen must rid themselves of mundane possessions.

From the day Constance accepted Madame Blavatsky's invitation, she spent long periods of time with her and became a Theosophist. She was aware that this Russian woman had such great knowledge about "the invisible part" of Nature, as only very few human beings have. She realized that the sincere adepts improved so much on the human evolutionary scale, as to fuse their personality with the Sixth Principle of the Universe or Universal Christ. It seems that Theosophy is a mixture of Christianity and Hinduism, but the main belief being in the intercourse between man and spirit. The most distinguished adepts are individuals who are actively involved with paranormal phenomena and are mediums.

Constance tells us that Madame Blavatsky herself often gave exhibitions using psychoelectrical power. She used to see whole passages of books which were not at hand, not even near her. "Such visions," Constance says, "often show the inverted original image as it would be seen on a mirror, and though the words can be easily read if there is a little practice, and the general sense and contents help to avoid serious mistakes, it is much more difficult when dealing with numbers . . ."

Don't you think that Madame Blavatsky would have been, if she had had the opportunity, a magnificent subject for psychophotography? Or don't you think that her faculties could have been measured by more scientific means today?

The Russian clairvoyant, according to her secretary's report, used to leave her physical body and enter astral space. Constance once heard a continued striking on the table by Madame Blavatsky's bed. Another time, the lamp that was in the same room suddenly turned on by itself. She thought that all these phenomena were due to spirits called *chelas,* which looked after the physical body of Madame Blavatsky while her astral body was absent. She verified this one evening when the striking was so constant and the light intermission so frequent, that she decided to wake up the Theosophist, who when recovering consciousness told her in a very excited way: "My heart! My heart! Why have you made me come back?" She gave her a dose of digitalis and reassured her. This was the dangerous way, Constance learned, to bring back a medium who was traveling in astral space; if done suddenly it could prove fatal.

Madame Blavatsky probably showed Constance her clairvoyance, in the sense of knowing the future, the day she asked her why she did not sell her house in Sweden, so that she would not have to worry about anything and could devote herself to Theosophy. Constance, who had been working with Madame Blavatsky for just a short time, stated that she did not want to give up her house. The Russian insisted, "The Master told me to let you know that if you sell your house immediately you will not have any loss; you will avoid a lot of troubles if you do it right away." Constance did not pay attention to her and wrote in her book, ". . . she wants me to sell my property, in order to have me even more bounded to Theosophy. My friends write me letters from many places saying that she is an old intriguer woman who is *psychologizing* me and uses the name of the Master to make me do what she wishes. This is a good chance to show her that I can keep my will completely free . . ." Later on, she repented when discovering that if the property would have been sold on that occasion, she would have made a huge profit. After many disturbances and troubles she sold it at a great loss. Perhaps this was only due to the major awareness of reality the Russian had.

Though I expect that you know my other books, I think this is the proper time to insist on something which I stated in one of them, *Beliefs and Their Engrammes,* related to this matter.

Spiritism is a belief which a large number of persons follow because it is based on the conviction that our activities go farther than matter, since we have been created by the lively spirit of the Creator, and, having been a part of matter during life, we still act after death, causing some phenomena that have come to pass from time immemorial. I already discussed parapsychology in that essay, underlining that even in matters not clear enough, spiritism—and Theosophy—are beliefs worthy of remark, though not being true in all their manifestations.

On the other hand, I stated before in *Beliefs and Their Engrammes* that it is a truth that a person may know the subconscious of another one, this being a cerebral function, no doubt, even if we do not know yet its location in the brain, nor its mechanism.

The phenomenon called "cerebral waves" or cerebral activity, when it reaches certain electric potentials of a certain quality, can be recorded by the electroencephalograph, but it may happen as in the case of X rays that the detected ones were only a part of a greater number of radiations with different kinds of characteristics, but still being radiations.

From October, 1974, date of publication of *Beliefs and Their Engrammes,* I not only did a lot of thinking, but I have researched it, assuming that the brain creates waves, and I wondered how or through what process this emission takes place. In other words, what antenna is used by this wonderful apparatus? I concluded that such an antenna is formed by neurovascular sensitive cells that are found at the base of the nails and called "arteriovenous glomic anastomoses."

In addition to the knowledge offered by the science called parapsychology, I still do think that the survival of the spirit, considered as an energy, would help us to understand not only clairvoyance, telepathy, and premonitions, but all great inspirations of geniuses who think and reason in a different way, performing associations and connections to their cerebral engrammes.

# 4

# DIVINATION, HOROSCOPES, SCIENCE FICTION

I have already said that divination is a very old practice, known by the Chinese, Hindus, Greeks, Aztecs, and almost all peoples of the world, and it is still being performed among persons of all cultural levels.

Chiromancy was performed by the Chinese, in 3,000 B.C., who used to read not only the palm of the hand but the sole of the foot. Nowadays it still has supreme value and even with its lack of scientific basis, there are sometimes amazing results. We find here again that hands and feet are basic elements of paranormal practices which have no satisfactory explanation yet. These are practices where there is neither trickery nor fraud involved.

When discussing divination, we have to bear in mind the atavistic predisposition to credibility, coming from old predicting practices; but the accurate knowledge that many graphologists and chiromantics have of the past and sometimes of the future of some people avoids imputing wrong beliefs to those who apply them. In this case, as well as in those of telling fortunes by leftover coffee grinds or tea leaves, or cases of cartomancy, we can only talk of beliefs that are not proved at all and risk the hypothesis of parapsychological phenomena existence, especially telepathy and clairvoyance, in the part that is already proven.

Graphology, according to Molly Freeman, is a generic term to mean all analysis of handwriting, but graphoanalysis is a specific scientific method applied to a document, and this is achieved by studies performed by the International Society of Graphoanalysis, which awards a diploma accrediting the student as a graphologist. These skills are now being used by corporations, schools, and associations to appraise, accept, or refuse job applicants or pupils. Several courses on this subject are taught at universities across the country.

Besides the methods of divination already pointed out, there are other ones, all of them identified by the suffix *mancy,* which in Greek means "divination." Oneiromancy or divination by means of dreams, could be said to be the prediction of the future of a person by interpretation of his dreams.

This means of knowing the future is as old as it is new. You will remember the biblical passage in which the Prophet Daniel interprets Nebuchadnezzar's dreams; it was he who had already ordered the death of all Chaldean magicians because they were not able to explain to him what he had dreamed. Daniel had a vision in which the arcanum was revealed to him, so the verdict against the magicians was changed and Daniel was taken to the king. The prophet told Nebuchadnezzar that he would interpret his dream not by his own means, but because the Lord had revealed it to him. He talked about the statue that had a head made out of gold, the chest and arms of silver, the womb and thighs of copper, the legs of iron, and the feet of clay. A stone tore off the mount and broke down the statue. Daniel explained that as the statue was made out of different materials, thus would the kingdoms of the world "until the God of Heavens will set up a kingdom that will not ever be destroyed and this kingdom will not pass to other nations, but will repeal and annihilate all these kingdoms and it will survive eternally." (Dan. 2:44).

Therefore, I say this is new because, according to psychoanalytic theories, dreams reveal, if not the future in an objective way, the changes that take place within ourselves in a subjective way if, according to Freud, we know how to interpret them and discover or, even more, listen to their calls for attention.

In addition to what we have seen and said of cases of premonition and telepathy, some dreams are definite and eloquent by themselves. They do not have room for doubt about their contents, as they are clearly admonitions.

In ancient times, the soothsayers studied the flight of birds to discover the future, or they studied the bowels of animals, or the movement of the waters of rivers. Nowadays they use the crystal ball or cups of coffee and tea. All these procedures are not under the rule of parapsychology because they depend on external elements, strange to both the soothsayer and the subject of divination. One wonders what accounts for their efficiency in so many cases.

I should say it is due to the interrelation between the soothsayer and the interested subject; the brain of the latter has gathered and kept his full story in his engrammes, and he unconsciously transfers it to the soothsayer, who computes it when it reaches his brain and puts it into words, using as a reinforcer what he projects on the objects he employs. This would be telepathy at a very short distance.

Salvador Freixedo says that all these objects "are nothing but *triggers* of the unconscious, which is the one that really foresees." Anyway, it is necessary to be cautious with all these procedures and, rather, avoid making use of them. Freixedo seems to understand this mechanism in a way that agrees with my own theory.

Another method of divination, which is very odd, is radiesthesy, which consists of waving a pendulum in front of the person whose future is going to be predicted. Possibly the pendulum, as a prolongation of the fingers that are holding it, extends the orders received from the brain to the tips of the fingers, becoming a more or less conscious way of comprehension.

During this procedure, the soothsayer or radiesthetician notices in advance if a movement of the pendulum going to the right means "yes" and another one to the left means "no," or vice versa. He immediately starts to ask questions, usually about the place where a treasure or another object is hidden and the pendulum moves, giving answers by going in a certain direction. The person who uses the pendulum must relax his arm so as not to give it any movement. Moreover, and according to those who know this method of divination, he must have a natural sensibility which no amount of practice would give him; it must be innate. In other words, his efficiency will depend on the number and quality of the vascular sensitive nervous cells he has.

Perhaps divination, more than any other method, lacking a

common or scientific explanation, is susceptible not only to mockery, but to fraud. At the International Congress of Parapsychology held in Mexico City, Dr. Bender told of a case where 2,000 marks was stolen from a poor man. He called the police, but they could not find the thief. The man was very upset and decided to ask the advice of a soothsayer, and he knew who had stolen the money. It had been taken by a boy who lived near him and whose description had been given by the soothsayer. The man filed a complaint against the boy, but the family filed a countercharge of fraud against the soothsayer.

Despite this, people of all cultural levels are still adepts in fortune-telling practices, and a proof of it is the tendency of wanting to know the horoscope sign of everyone they meet. Most newspapers and magazines encourage this fondness, and almost no one ignores his zodiac forecast, which depends on his date of birth, and there are many people who read what the horoscope predicts for the day before they even read the news.

This belief in the horoscope is explained first by the atavism in modern men's minds; predisposition to the established engrammes prevails, as it did in primitive people's minds. The worship of the stars in ancient days makes people of today feel linked to a certain constellation in the zodiac, or to look for the key to their destiny on the planet that rules during the time of his birth. Second, horoscopes always have at least one statement which flatters the reader, either on his personal way of acting or related to his near future; this facilitates the belief in the horoscope and its acceptance. Third, we almost always talk of coincidences that give verisimilitude to horoscopes and not of the instances which may prove their inaccuracy, and that is why they are thought to be efficient in predicting the future. The credibility granted to the horoscope is a false but healthy belief that can be corrected, if we accept the explanation given by an educated person.

There are studies on this subject, however, that maintain the accuracy of the horoscope. Michel Gauquelin, in his book *Cosmic Clocks,* offers us mathematical proofs of the influence stars have on the mental and physical formation of individuals.

Gauquelin computed the horoscopes of more than 500 physicians, and he expected each of these horoscopes to be very different. He was amazed when he found that Saturn and Mars, the planets which according to traditional astrology govern the medical profession, were set in a position that favored such horoscopes at a greater rate than the one that could be based on an estimation of probabilities. He repeated his experiment with another 500 physicians and again found that Mars and Saturn were in the same favorable position, at a greater rate than the one allowed by the laws of statistics. He was then convinced that the presence of Saturn and Mars in the horoscopes of physicians was more than coincidence. According to Gauquelin, physicians not only chose their career because they were born on a certain date, but because it was already written in their genetic writing or what he called, their "planetary inheritance."

Gauquelin accomplished many other studies on persons of different professions, and his results always corroborated his initial findings.

Paranormal phenomena are not limited to scientific study; they have invaded the arts, especially literature. Science fiction, also called "improbabilia," seems to be coming closer to the truth every day. Even in countries like Spain and Mexico, where technology has not reached a great degree of development, the novels and tales of science fiction have great popular appeal.

It is also said that the works of this kind are no longer outer-space adventures, with cowboys dressed as astronauts and Indians dressed as Martians, as they were some years before; nowadays they are a wonderful window to the future, the greatest and the most illuminating we have available, and through which we can examine man and the positive and negative features of civilization created by him, from the picture of homo sapiens in prehistoric caves and holding tools of bone and weapons of stone, to the world of the future.

Actually, science fiction offers sociological, psychological, and even anthropological insights.

Some of the adventures described are unrealistic, however, and even grotesque; sometimes only a few of them stimulate the reader's imagination in a literary or thought-provoking way. There is a great difference between anticipating what our world would be like in twenty-five or fifty years and that there will be scheduled flights from Earth to all points of the solar system and the stars. True and worthwhile science fiction actually anticipates scientific progress without exaggerating it, as did Jules Verne in his novel *From the Earth to the Moon.* It may be said that it is impossible to evaluate the worth of science fiction because its quality depends on whether or not the predicted events come to pass. The same can be said for prophets, who cannot be considered as such if their prophecies do not come true, or if clairvoyants' predictions do not occur.

A tale which I consider science fiction is one entitled *The Sixth Sense,* by the Mexican poet Amado Nervo. In this novella, the protagonist has a brain operation which allows him to foresee the future. Nervo emphasizes the destiny of his protagonist, paying small attention to generalizations. The most important part of the tale is the lesson: if we could know the future, the poet says, all the evil and unpleasantness to occur, and, above all, the date of our death, we would live in perpetual fear, plunged in the most terrible anguish, just like that suffered by a person tied to a railroad track and watching a train coming at him. If our future is bright, if we are to find true happiness, prior knowledge of our destiny (and, therefore, the lack of surprise) will make it spiritless. This happens to the protagonist of *The Sixth Sense.* His life vacillates between worry and fear.

Another tale dealing with foreseeing the future is *Enoch Soames,* by the English critic Max Beerbohm. The hero, Enoch, is an optimistic writer who does not accept his limitations and always dreams of fortune and fame. He is so sure he will be immortalized that he sells his soul to the Devil on the condition that he will be able to come back to this world a hundred years after his death and see his name in the Library of the British Museum. He dies and his spirit goes to the museum, but he sees that he has been forgotten, his name appears in neither anthologies nor papers, not even in a simple catalogue.

These two cases show how some writers view the ability to

see into the future and whether the gift proves to be a help or a hindrance. Obviously they feel it is better not to know our destiny. I agree with them to a certain extent. Of course, if the future revealed is favorable, it is easy to want to know more.

I will tell you of a strange incident that happened where I was the protagonist. On Jalapa Street, in Mexico City, there is a cafeteria where a man tells the future from the leftover coffee grinds in a person's cup. That soothsayer told me I was going to take a long trip, which I did. This is not rare, because travel is usually predicted for everyone, but he added that on a faraway island I was going to find a ring that had belonged to a physician who was famous in that region, and it would bring me good luck. After visiting several islands, a very old ring caught my attention when I was at a bazaar in Bali. I remembered what the soothsayer had told me, moreover because he had added, "Get it, by any means." I tried to buy it but the price was too high. I left the bazaar, and I was so deeply impressed that I returned the next day. The owners would not lower the price, but they agreed to exchange the ring for my Polaroid camera and a large supply of film that I had brought with me. At last I had the ring, which actually brought good luck because I have since received great encouragement to carry on my organic theory on parapsychological phenomena. I verified, as well, that the ring had belonged to a well-known physician who had passed away a long time ago. The prediction had come to pass.

## MIRACULOUS HEALINGS

Our now familiar Constance Wachtmeister refers to a certain occasion when Madame Blavatsky became seriously ill. Two physicians were treating her, and one of them, a Belgian, said that he had never known of a case like hers where a person suffered so seriously with kidney trouble as this patient did and still lived. He was fairly convinced that he could do nothing to save her. Dr. Ellis verified that a person as ill as she was lucky to be alive.

Madame Gebbard, an old friend of the Theosophist, suggested that Madame Blavatsky write her last will and testament.

She did so, leaving all her possessions, meager though they were, to Constance.

The secretary, writing in her book, said she became horrified one day when she first perceived that "peculiar though faint smell of death that often precedes the dissolution of human body." She could not accept the idea of Madame Blavatsky's passing away without concluding her book. She expected something very likely to a miracle, as two years before, in Aydar, the clairvoyant would have died if she had not been kept alive by occult means, when she made the supreme decision of living and working for those who had still to come into contact with the teachings of the Theosophic Society.

All night long she looked after her employer with great care, but weariness got the better of her at dawn. She awoke with a start, fearing that Madame Blavatsky had died without her realizing, but to her joy and surprise, the Russian was perfectly well and told her, "The Master has been here. He gave me the choice between dying and getting free if I wanted to, or living to conclude *The Secret Doctrine*." She knew great suffering marked her way—physical, because of her illness, and moral, because of the slander and verbal attack she always endured and which would grow even worse; but she wanted to live to finish her book.

When the doctors came to see Madame Blavatsky, they were amazed that she was still alive, and they were never able to account for her miraculous recovery.

Minou Drouet, a gifted girl in literature, tells us about being in Marcel Castellier's house, where she met Francis de Miomandre, whom she felt was unfortunately forgotten. She felt he deserved the Goncourt prize for his wonderful book *Escrit sur de l'eau*. It was a time when the members of the Goncourt jury were clairvoyants. When they felt Francis's hand on theirs, they entered a strangely fascinating universe.

The first time Minou went to Castellier's house she knew it was important that the fireplace in the living room be lit in order for everyone to be able to give of themselves. During this visit to Mozart Avenue, Miomandre showed her a precious jewel whose molecules seeemed to form part of the fantastic kingdom of *The Above.*

Another evening, while she was visiting Marcel, she told Francis she wanted to touch his forehead. He got close to her and said that his head ached, and when she put her hands on his temples she laughed and said, "It could be said that there is heavy traffic in here, as in the street."

The next morning she received a phone call from Marcel Castellier saying that Miomandre had suffered a terrible hemorrhage shortly after she left. When the doctor came, he said that the hemorrhage had saved him from death.

There are cases of healings which cannot be explained scientifically. These then fall into the realm of religious faith.

"And a certain woman, which had an issue of blood twelve years, And had suffered many things of many physicians, and had spent all that she had, and was nothing bettered, but rather grew worse, When she had heard of Jesus, came in the press behind, and touched his garment. For she said, If I may touch but his clothes, I shall be whole. And straightway the fountain of her blood was dried up; and she felt in her body that she was healed of that plague. And Jesus, immediately knowing in himself that virtue had gone out of him, turned him about in the press, and said, Who touched my clothes? And his disciples said unto him, Thou seest the multitude thronging thee, and sayest thou, Who touched me? And he looked round to see her that had done this thing. But the woman fearing and trembling, knowing what was done in her, came and fell down before him, and told him all the truth. And he said unto her, Daughter, thy faith hath made thee whole; go in peace and be whole of thy plague (Mark 5:25-34).

Dr. Salvador García Doreste, parapsychology teacher at Universidad Iberoamericana, and who was a member of the International Congress on the subject held in Mexico City in December 1974, spoke about the miracles and told the newspapermen that parapsychology had shown that the so-called "miracles" which were imputed to many saints were only phenomena created by man either in the state of autosuggestion or in one of intensive telepathy. Christ, for instance, needed no supernatural power to heal a blind or crippled man because in some cases, the sicknesses were psychosomatic, and it was only necessary to use autosuggestion to accomplish the so-called healing. Some persons believe that these phenomena are true miracles, Dr. Doreste insists, including the miracles of Lourdes and Fatima. When these cases are investigated, it is discovered that autosuggestion or intense telepathy were involved. Generally speaking about parapsychology, Dr. Doreste feels we all have parapsychological faculties, and even those with a more acute faculty can have mental disturbances because of their mental avidity.

If we could explain all these paranormal, and to a certain extent, unexplainable phenomena, they would no longer be considered miracles. If it were possible to demonstrate that the brain is capable of creating energy, and conveying it through the nervous cells forming solenoid fibers around the vascular system, these acting as antenna, then other phenomena could be explained in the same way, as the case of the biblical woman with the hemorrhage.

We must bear in mind that not all the healings considered miracles are a consequence of phenomena clearly classified as paranormal. Salvador Freixedo tells us that medicine assumes that such healings come either from illusory afflictions or are due to the influence of the mind over the body. However, the explanation becomes much more difficult when the method of healing is not spiritual or intangible, but by means of something material, like a knife or a pair of scissors.

Freixedo has witnessed in Brazil arduous operations on every organ of the body—operations performed without any anesthesia or antiseptic.

During one such operation, an eye doctor urged the patient to have faith in Christ, made an act of faith, and then with a pair of scissors started to cut, without any preparation or anesthesia, a film on the eye which was covering half of the pupil. The patient nervously closed the eye each time he saw the scissors draw near, but this did not prevent the doctor from making the cut that skillfully separated the fleshiness covering the pupil. Using only the handle of the instrument and in a very rough manner, he removed some fibers or enlarged tissues from the rear part of the eye of the patient who had suffered for a long time. It took only seconds to do.

He was not only a witness to these operations, but was also the patient during a very difficult one, performed by a man who knew nothing about medicine; he was a bricklayer, and Freixedo says he has been feeling much better because of the operation.

Freixedo's experience cannot be classified under parapsychological phenomena, even if he does use three or four cases as examples, including his own. When I was in Havana, I diagnosed a cerebral tumor located in the frontal region of a patient. She had an operation and recovered the sight that she had lost some months before, and she stopped acting disturbed and insane. Many people thought of it as a miraculous healing. This is not true at all, of course. Diagnosis was made by a cerebral angiography, which was a procedure fully unknown in Cuba at the time, and the operation was performed according to a fairly simple technique. (See my autobiography, *A Doctor's Odyssey*.)

Paracelsus said that though the object of your faith is true or false, you will always obtain the same results. Faith, indeed, in a very wide sense, and not exactly religious, may be such an important element that it would be fully necessary to recover lost health. To this point of view, virtue itself would have certain relics, some amulets, the waters of a certain place to work like the spells of a sorcerer.

American psychologist Parker emphasizes the therapeutic value of prayer not as a miraculous panacea, but as a scientific method with effects on the subconscious. To a great extent, this is the cause, he feels, of illnesses such as asthma, hay fever, and high blood pressure. According to the theory of psychosomatic illnesses, these sicknesses start as functional troubles in the subconscious and become organic afflictions which a great deal of physicians treat based on the symptoms without bearing in mind other causes.

From Parker's point of view, four basic personality disturbances are at the bottom of all afflictions of the subconscious: fear, hate, guilt, and a feeling of inferiority. Parker, through experiments performed in Redlands University, discovered and faced these basic problems, advising the patient to pray, and, in many cases, it resulted in his recovery.

## THE SIXTH SENSE AS A MENTAL POWER: TRUSTING IN YOURSELF

In this chapter, we will dwell on the sixth sense, its spectacular and mysterious manifestations, and its meaning, which is somewhat vague, especially when people refer to somebody as having a sixth sense.

Some people studying the subject of the power of the mind compare mental power to certain paranormal abilities of human beings.

Happiness in this life or in the hereafter is the goal we all want to attain (consciously or not). Much of the advice, if not all, thinkers of the ages have given to obtain that goal could be stated in one simple phrase: Trust in yourself. This trust involves faith, optimism, and self confidence. These encompass hope, control of thoughts and actions, good mental organization, and an attitude of benevolence toward other people. Remarkably enough, the traits are not always exhibited by those succeeding in this world.

People who have faith are those who trust in themselves. Those not trusting their own forces, but discouraging easily in the face of trouble, lacking energy and the will to win, and doubting their ability to succeed will never accomplish anything. Have you ever noticed that people who are sure of themselves receive the acceptance of the crowd? People follow them wherever they go in order to help them achieve their goals even if, as in many cases, those "magnetic" persons are less intelligent or have inferior personalities when compared with those who serve them. They trust these people and their own faith in them, and that is why they have no doubt that victory is around the corner. Without man's intense drive to rule nature and other men, culture, knowledge, and wealth would be of no use. It is man's enthusiasm which gives him a reason to act and makes it easy for him to manipulate other persons who are attracted to him without their realizing it.

In every aspect of human existence, the man who trusts himself and inspires confidence in others is the one who succeeds and is immortalized, becoming an example to his fellowman. When we are not sure of ourselves and do not trust our own power, lack of both iniative and enthusiasm defeats us, and we cannot achieve our goal. Ideas fail to enlighten or stimulate us, success does not come our way, and we fail, victims of our own diffidence, our doubts and hesitation, our indecision and fear.

If we analyzed the lives of great men we would see that they accomplished their tasks because they were helped, above all, by an unlimited and strong confidence in themselves and by a firm conviction that what they were doing was right. They acted as if nothing could resist their push and nobody dared stop their progress. Thus they reached their goals and triumphed because they concentrated the best of their spirit on their work.

However, what has been told in general terms does not always agree with fact. I know, from my own experience, that professional jealousy can create obstacles for us; we must not be discouraged, bearing in mind that logic and truth will always triumph. It is sad to think that the lack of confidence in oneself can cause the failure and ruin of others.

There are people gifted with ability, ambition, knowledge, and good health, but who sink into darkness and oblivion because they lacked enthusiasm. It is very difficult to find a person who has succeeded in life without enthusiasm for all his activities, and without the firm conviction that he would, sooner or later, triumph. Almost all people who are defeated in life are distinguished by their indolence, apathy, shyness, limited observation skills, lack of concentration, fear without an apparent cause, and, of course, by one or many bad habits.

Relying on others is relatively easier than relying on oneself. It facilitates the achievement of acts that would otherwise be impossible to perform on one's own because of the lack of preparation in a certain area or in a certain subject. It is not possible to have a knowledgeable control of all the arts and sciences at one time. Everyone must have his own course of study.

Those wishing to have confidence in themselves must make a mental and spiritual effort to organize their minds to fight and not to be discouraged in the face of obstacles, nor to become impatient when the fight is a long and hard one. They must believe that success will be the result of their efforts to increase their knowledge, to achieve perfection in the arts, to obtain utmost skill in their professions, or whatever it is they desire.

It is necessary that people free their minds of all causes of restlessness and anxiety, and that they assume, by concentration, control of their thoughts and concentrate them on a single goal, to learn how to apply the will properly and to perceive, by intuition, the unlimited power of the mind. But we should bear in mind that this goal must not come from selfishness or from vanity. Envy and hate rise from one's insecurity. The envious are almost always those who have failed, and those who hate or systematically criticize everything are those who have a weak character.

The sophistication of modern life has given rise to man's trying to succeed through abjection, having the easiest ways as his means and rejecting dignity, afraid of hard work and constancy. Men do not want to know anything about *will, energy,* or *mental power,* stating doctorally and without any reason that they are merely hindrances, and they devote themselves to pecuniary triumphs, considering money as the clearest and most valuable asset in life.

In today's schools, homes, and churches, people are not taught to trust themselves, to educate their character, to rule their will, to, in a word, discover the wonderful source of their inner powers. Thus, most of today's youth, instead of directing their age to progress, degenerate into easy pleasures, into corrupt politics, and even into vice. Respect for society cannot be earned, nor a good work performed, if there is no conviction of the goodness of our acts, and if there is no inspiration in an ideal of improvement or even of perfection, should it be necessary.

Many successful people are accused of being inhuman, vulgar, rude, and unscrupulous; but, truly, it is undeniable that great financiers, remarkable statesmen, eminent scientists, discoverers of continents, invincible warriors, devoted reformers and seers, visionary apostles—these men did not set aside their ideals to handle trivial problems, nor were they stopped by prejudices of any kind; they were devoted enthusiastically to their work, without thinking of anything but the success of their cause. They were brave enough to face danger and strong enough to face threats. On the contrary, many scholars, ministers of state, and counselors were left behind, stopped by shyness and doubt and maybe dazzled by fruitless and selfish dreams.

Unfortunately, it is a characteristic of human nature to give to the wealthy person and to take from the one who lacks even the most necessary things for a decent life. The more one owns, the more he is offered, and poor people are denied everything. Of course, it is an unfair attitude, but in our social organization, justice does not seem a basic characteristic. If men cannot find the way to solidarity, they will encourage the ones placed in an upper level and push down those on a lower level. Therefore, people who are sure of themselves are *magnetic;* they attract and subdue all others. People are touched by good feelings when such magnetic people pass by; their optimism can be felt and they are admired; they shower peacefulness and reassurance wherever they go because they have these qualities within themselvs. They have courage not only for their personal profit, but they give it as well to the communities through which they pass.

Just as good health can be recovered if one believes that sickness is only a passing obstacle whose effects will disappear soon if the desire to be healed is added to the aid of medicine, wisdom can be more easily gained if one believes that the search for knowledge and the character of benevolence are the so-called magic keys to serenity and the strength to face not only injustice and displeasure, but death itself.

Insecure people blame bad luck for their errors in judgment and their ineptitude to face obstacles. It is urgent for these persons to change their mental attitude: instead of thinking of failure and impotence, they must discover their own capabilities and qualities (everyone has at least one good trait) and improve and develop them.

Those who pay attention to the surface only, without delving to the bottom of things, do not understand the rationale or extent of faith. We are coping again with the phenomenon of Babelism because the word "faith" is not given its actual meaning or it is only given one of many. Faith is the firm belief in something that could be God, the beginning of all existing things, or the power that is in the stars, in the elements, in the animals, or in Man. Faith, therefore, can be religious, scientific, or psychological in nature. Depending on the individual's mentality as to the choice of a certain faith constituting a guide, what is essential is to have faith, period.

The person who has faith is usually an optimist in the strongest sense of the word. He does not doubt his own abilities and, more important, he has no negative thoughts and feelings which could destroy his inner well-being and his environment. He does not criticize, gossip, or do any ill toward others.

Optimism is a natural consequence of good mental and physical health, a kind and tolerant nature, and, in many cases, a true love of God. True peace of mind is the first prerequisite for optimism. It is certain that God has gifted us with inner powers which we are capable of developing in order to improve ourselves and our lives in every aspect.

## THE POWER OF THE SUBCONSCIOUS

Some psychologists have considered that though we only have one physical mind, it has two parts remarkably different and which may be independent or synchronized. These are the objective and subjective minds. For these psychologists, Dr. Joseph Murphy included, the objective mind acts through the five traditional senses: sight, hearing, smell, taste, and touch. Through these we enter into contact with the world and our fellowman. According to many psychologists, the objective mind is the one which observes, experiments, reasons, and is educable.

The subjective mind comes into contact with the environment by means other than the five traditional senses.

It may be called *intuition* or the *subconscious,* but it could be called the *sixth sense.* The subconscious settles the emotions and carries on its most important duties while the five objective senses are resting. The subconscious mind "sees without using the eyes," it is clairvoyant, clairaudient, and telepathic. The subjective mind is docile to suggestion and can be controlled in this manner. Anything occurring to a person remains impressed in his subconscious. According to these ideas, if you, for example, have said many times that you do not like mussels, the day you have them you will be sick because your subconscious will remember that you dislike them. If you think that you cannot sleep after drinking a cola, it will be so because your subconscious will obey the suggestion.

The Egyptians, Chaldeans, and Babylonians realized the existence of the subconscious, although they did not give it that name; they believed it was where the heart was situated. This belief lasted through the centuries, and it is still common to hear that something is "an impulse of the heart," referring to something we know is certain by who knows what mysterious means. Nowadays we have learned that the history of the universe is impressed not only in the subconscious, but in every single cell of our organism (at least in the individual as an element of a species).This would explain, in part, the latent knowledge we have about all things, but in many cases we do not appreciate it because the external confuses us and deflects us from our inner and congenital wisdom.

Dr. Murphy advises that if you wish a healing, for example, go to a silent place, breathe calmly, do not let your attention wander, think of the healing power of your subconscious, state that the sick organ is getting well in this very moment. When doing this there must be no resentment or bitterness in your heart; everybody must be forgiven. This process of healing may be repeated three or four times a day. Remember that your subconscious has created the state your body is in, and it is capable of healing it. However, many people who try this say, "I am getting worse; I will never be well. My sickness is serious." This negative mental attitude neutralizes the positive attitude. If the surgeon who has removed an appendix opens the wound again to see how it is, and half an hour later opens it once more, he will probably cause septicemia. In the same way, you will destroy or avoid your healing by always having negative thoughts. What Dr. Murphy says agrees in many respects with some principles of Christian Science.

Indeed, we must learn how to use the unquestionable power of subconscious, in the same way we have learned how to harness atomic power and electricity through the knowledge of their laws and properties.

Many great men (Marconi, Edison, Ford, Einstein) have had interior visions which have given them the necessary knowledge to achieve their goal in science, industry, or the arts. Scientific research has shown that the ability of making the subconscious work has determined the success of some important discoverers and remarkable artists. Most psychologists state that all human beings have that "huge inner dynamo" and that we can use it at our will if we know how.

Neuroanatomopathologists Fernando de Castro and Isaac Costero have described nerve fibers and nervous cells unevenly distributed in the adventitia of arteries, as well as the arteriovenous glomic anastomoses which are found more frequently at the bottom of the fingernails and those found in the carotid sinus as affecting the subconscious. They have observed, as well, that such cells vary in number, distribution, and general aspect from individual to individual.

It is an undeniable fact that the subconscious is constantly at work. Sometimes we spend all day trying to solve a problem and find no solution. We decide then to put it aside for a while, sleep, and when we awaken we suddenly come up with a satisfactory way of solving it. Another example of this is when we are used to waking up at seven, but on a certain day we have to be ready at five because we are leaving on a trip; before the alarm clock rings we are already awake. It is the subconscious that has awakened us at the right time. This is also true when we must give medicine to a person close to us, and we awaken in time to accomplish this task.

The objective mind or conscious usually hinders the job of the subjective mind or subconscious because it uses the five senses to render judgment based on external aspects only. This places us under the rule of false beliefs, fears, and opinions that lack a reasonable basis, but which register in the subconscious, preparing it psychologically and emotionally in such a way that we have to act according to what it has been shown. It is as a computer, working according to what has been programmed in it.

But the subconscious cannot work in a profitable way for the individual if he is tense and anxious. It is necessary to be relaxed, patient, to think of the problem as if already solved, no matter whether the trouble is related to health, money, or work. We have to remember that feeling is the clue of every subconscious demonstration; so it is necessary to receive enthusiastically the present idea, as if we were achieving it and feeling comfort within us.

Murphy compares the subconscious to a bank and advises us to make steady deposits in that "internal bank," deposits of peace, harmony, faith, and hope, and they will be multiplied a thousand times, and the "interest" will be in the form of prosperity and happiness. If our reactions to daily problems are impatience, bitterness, criticism, and resentment, these are what will be deposited in our internal bank. If we need force, faith, and confidence, it would be impossible to take them out, as such deposits were never made.

Murphy's comparison is much easier to understand if it is explained in terms of engrammes. If you face a difficult decision, or have a problem that cannot be easily solved, stay calm; completely relax your muscles and concentrate your attention on solving the problem in a logical way. Get a pencil and a paper and write down all the possibilities your mind can find; concentrate on how happy you would be if you could find a perfect solution. If you feel that your attention wanders, start again. When reaching this state, which I call "the threshold of hypnosis," choose the best solution from the ideas you have written. Eliminate the following ideas—"Things are getting worse," "I will never get the answer," "I do not know how to get out of the trouble," "There is no hope"—otherwise you will be undoing the good work already accomplished. When thinking of the solution, the brain will work the way it should.

Franklin D. Roosevelt said that the only thing we have to fear is fear itself, and it is, indeed, one of the most terrible burdens to carry through a lifetime, especially when one has fears and knows not of what. There are many things of which people are afraid—pain, illness, death, loss of material possessions or social position, war, violence, disasters resulting from man and nature (earthquakes, floods, fires, droughts). Maybe the most harmful of all is fear of oneself, that terror of which we have already spoken and which manifests itself in insecurity and weakness. Self-confidence, the power of the subconscious, or positive autosuggestion—no matter what you call it—it is absolutely necessary to find some means of conquering such fears.

There are many cases where singers, orators, lecturers, or actors get terrified when facing an audience, especially if it is their debut. They feel an unreasonable fear which makes them stutter, be out of tune, or become so tense that their acting suffers. A good way to fight fear is to relax two or three times a day when alone, breathing slowly and deeply, and imagining that one is acting so well and naturally that the audience is attentive and enthusiastic. After a while the fear will disappear.

Every time fear arises without apparent cause, it is necessary to think of the opposite, i.e. peacefulness and success, because if our mind is busy with just the idea of fear, obsessions and complexes could take over. The key to eliminating certain fears is to think positive thoughts.

An extraordinary example of the power of the mind was told by Dr. Hubert Larcher, whom I met at the International Congress of Parapsychology in Mexico City in 1974. He told us about being a prisoner in a concentration camp during the Second World War. He fought cold and hunger by using mental concentration, practically becoming like a hibernating animal, like a mole or a marmot. He was able to lower his body temperature at will, using less calories, diminishing hunger as well. He survived while hundreds of his friends starved and froze to death in the Nazi concentration camp. This is a perfect example of the fantastic power of which the mind is capable when one knows how to use it.

## HOW TO PROFIT BY OUR EXTRASENSORY PERCEPTION

Harold Sherman, an expert on parapsychology and president of the ESP Research Associates Foundation, wrote five books on this subject. Dr. Sherman has not only fully researched paranormal phenomena, but has experimented on himself, giving his works an uncommon worth. He has written two more books, working together with other American researchers.

Dr. Sherman says that the air surrounding us is full of vibrations from radio and television which we are unable to see or hear until we bring them where our sight and ear can perceive them and are transformed into images and sound by mechanical means. We are told that the human body is a transmitter and receiver. Scientists suggested recently the possibility of each cell of the body containing not only an adaptation of its specific function, but a recorder of everything happening. It is conceivable then that intelligence beyond our comprehension enters into all forms of life, from the infinitely small to the infinitely large.

I agree that the brain is an instrument which, like radio and television, converts not only the luminous and acoustic waves but infra or supra luminous and acoustic waves, into images and sound. But one must remember that radio and television use an antenna, and they would not work without one. I suggest that the vascular sensitive neurocells of the arterial system, mainly found at the bottom of the fingernails and in the carotid sinus, serve as an antenna for that marvelous transmitter and receiver called the brain. The root of my theory is based on this suggestion. Those cells may or may not contain, as stated by Sherman, a recording of all happenings.

Sherman emphasizes this undeniable fact: because we have memory, all concepts about God rose from the belief in supernatural acts. He thinks that in this modern age in which science has swept away superstition and ignorance, adepts of all religions should strive to verify the *reality* of the spiritual powers they follow. This proof, says Sherman, could be found only in and through the manifestation of what we call the power of extrasensory perception. If this power actually exists, and the proof of its existence is strong, its study and development are of the utmost importance and will be much more valuable than any research studying outer space and other worlds, on the problems of man on earth, on his true nature, and on his relation to his Creator.

Sherman speaks of premonitions that he has had and concludes that the conscious sensation of a real impression is different from one of fear or apprehension, and with practice, you will distinguish the difference among these feelings and recognize a genuine *heart impulse* when you have one. Then, he says, you must be brave and follow it. The latter is the most difficult step of all, as it may incur the ridicule of friends and relatives when you explain you simply feel you must (or must not, depending on the case) do this or that at a certain moment. It is impossible to explain a heart impulse or justify it. If it is a true one, deeds will prove it. But, he goes on, we are dealing with things that are beyond physics, in time and space, and the person who feels the heart impulse is ready to judge or to act according to it. There are also times when a heart impulse is not accurately received. (This same warning was issued by Paul Guth.)

In regard to clairvoyance and divination, Sherman states that we know the future exists for us in a way; a series of certain happenings will follow from this moment on, up to death, and maybe beyond. An infinite chain of happenings occurring during an inconceivable number of years, he continues, takes us to the moment of our individual birth. From this point, he emphasizes, nothing happens by chance. The universe is ruled by laws of cause and effect. As trivial and insignificant as something appears it has to have a cause.

This does not mean Sherman ascribes to determinism or fatalism, as he refutes them as follows: a person can predict, for instance, the crash of an airplane, but if a mechanic checks and repairs the engine before the departure, the *cause* of the crash will disappear and the plane will fly without a mishap. This will not diminish the value of the prediction, as the plane would have crashed had it remained in the condition the person making the prediction *saw* through extrasensory power. *Causality* acts on superior mental powers, before they become *effects* capable of being appreciated by the five physical senses, which, says Sherman, should explain why many seers are mistaken in their predictions. If they have real extrasensory abilities, people can feel something happening to somebody else, based on the present causalities of the moment. But other forces interfering after the prediction may change the causalities, altering or annulling what was predicted. This then seems to contradict what Sherman stated before when he said that if a heart impulse was real, events would prove it. Truth is truth and falsehood is falsehood—sooner or later, events will verify a truth.

So-called mystics, says Sherman, and prophets have foretold world happenings that sometimes have come true. On these occasions the conscious has been as strong and persistent as to keep a powerful basic causality. Minor powers opposing it have been vanquished or put aside, and the predicted happening occurred. This fact has caused learned men to remark that history tends to repeat itself, which is a way of saying that if humanity does not change its way of thinking and acting, it will go on attracting calamities again and again. I have said this many times.

In regard to dreams, Sherman thinks that extrasensory powers have a wide field of action through the kingdoms of the subconscious, having a sort of communication line and assisting the individual in all his activities when he sleeps. It seems that these powers would have an intelligence of their own and would pass into the individual as vivid dreams that are mental images and create deep feelings and stimulations, sometimes even spoken instructions being given in a dream.

One may dream and yet, without a belief in extrasensory

perception, never have such experiences. We must ask for help and guidance in acquiring faith. Sherman also says spiritual leaders emphasize the necessity of faith when praying, and that we need, as well, faith in our extrasensory powers if we want satisfactory results.

Allow me to refer to another interesting concept held by Sherman and relate it to my own theory on the organic basis of ESP. Sherman says that if man produces what he thinks, the combined thoughts of men, organized and centered in an object, this being constructive or destructive, must produce an effect whose nature will be the same as those thoughts. It is understandable, after knowing these facts, that a sensitive person can *syntonize* (Sherman's italics) especially when dreaming, with intensive areas of thoughts emitted by millions of creatures. Dr. Sherman emphasizes, by using the word *"syntonize,"* the possibility of the human brain being so sensitive to different kinds of energy that it could receive or transmit through an antenna made up of a network of vascular sensitive neurocells which extend all through the body.

Of healings achieved by faith Sherman says that when considering that a greater power within ourselves has built up the body we are in from the moment of its conception, and that that power must be still inside us, why doubt its capability to recreate any part of the body requiring repair because of a wound or sickness? He accepts that external factors have an influence on both the hurting and the healing of the body, but he insists on faith being essential for healing. However, he warns that some persons wrongly believe they must set aside medical aid if they want to use the healing powers of the mind, thinking that one or the other is to be used and not both. Actually, the average person becomes too tense when trying to activate his internal healing powers if trusting only in his faith, excluding any medical help. But, continues Sherman, faith in the doctor and in the treatment, together with faith in one's own healing power, can result in a positive, confident, and optimistic attitude, which will greatly contribute to one's recovery.

Another of Sherman's observations which is applicable to

extrasensory perception is that there is a great psychological value in the consciousness of a person concentrating on himself at a definite time. It is enough to stimulate a profitable reaction in both the mind and body of the receiver. But he knows, from his own experience, that something else besides thoughts is transmitted and received. He sometimes feels that all his energy is drained from him producing a reaction on the nervous centers of the scruff of the neck and the solar plexus. He has, at these times, to make a conscious effort to cut off the connection to get mental and physical relief.

In this discussion of the sixth sense, we have talked of aesthetic senses, suggestion, hypnotism, spiritism, premonitions, telepathy, clairvoyance, clairaudience, the occult, the invisible, faith, mental power, corporal expression, miraculous healings, and all related to the so-called sixth sense. The term "sixth sense" encompasses many aspects; this was the case with the word "colic." When asking the cause of somebody's death, the answer was almost always "colic." Little by little, that colic was specified as peritonitis, appendicitis, intestinal obstruction, thrombosis in the mesenteric artery, acute pancreatitis and so on. Of course, the word has been forgotten to the extent of not appearing in any medical treaties. I think the same will happen to the expression "sixth sense." Eventually all phenomena related to wonderful and enigmatic human power will be studied and demonstrated by science.

# 5

# OUR SIXTH SENSE: ORGANIC BASIS FOR ESP

Having devoted my whole life to the study of the nervous system and its functions, I am now at the point where I am able to present my own physical theory to explain paranormal phenomena.

I will try to show that the neurocells enervating the circulatory system are most likely the ones acting as part of an "antenna" receiving and transmitting the energy responsible for extrasensory perception. To actually demonstrate this, one would need precise instruments capable of detecting and registering even smaller microelectrodes and hypersensitive platismographs for energies of the ones that can be detected to date but with very fine results.

Just as the known sense organs receive stimuli from the outside and transmit them to the brain, which acts like a marvelous computer, so too the neurovascular elements forming the antenna also receive and transmit stimuli, producing these other perceptions in the brain.

Allow me to explain the elements of this antenna according to my theory.

First, around each artery there are accordion-like nerve fibers embedded into the layer of tissue (the adventitia) that covers the outside of the artery. The vascular system actually serves as a support for these highly sensitive specialized nerve fibers.

In the normal state of the vessel the coils can be seen as quite regularly spaced apart. But in vasodilation of the artery these coils are spread farther apart. In vasoconstriction they are brought much closer together. This is because these nerve fibers are not elastic, not capable of stretching in accordance with the

October, 1949, in which I reported two cases of great importance:

"We have observed two cases in which the angiograms[1] were normal in timing and normal anatomico-chronologically[2] but in which the opaque substance was passed from the arterial tree to the capillaries and from them to the inferior sagittal sinus and the great cerebral vein of Galen, and also to the middle cerebral vein. This is abnormal or at least infrequent because the blood customarily goes from the capillaries to the descending and ascending veins first. It is only one and one-half seconds after that stage that the blood reaches the abovementioned sinuses. To make ourselves clear, we should say that even if the whole circulatory sequence were in four and one-half seconds and anatomically there was no evidence of any abnormality, the pathway of blood was unusual, and that this abnormality may be related to the clinical findings [clinical history and angiogram]."

The known nervous mechanisms responsible for dilation and constriction of the arteries would be related to these three sections described above. This is apparent from the great number of connections they have throughout the nervous system.

I must repeat that it is in the brain that all our sensations are programmed, as well as the different kinds of perception and our experiences. This is so because of the engrammes placed by them in the brain. This is what makes the big difference between man and the animals, and, moreover, what according to my theory distinguishes man from MAN.

The brain consists of several regions functioning differently with interconnections among them on different levels. While we are performing voluntary acts, we are also performing involuntary ones at the same time. These are both automatically regulated and coordinated by the autonomic nervous system. The

---

[1]An angiogram is the visualization by means of X rays of the circulatory process of the brain taken in four and a half seconds to cover a complete exploration of its circulation using the Sanchez-Perez Seriograph.

[2]The above medical terms mean two different ways of the circulation of the blood in the brain, being that the infrequent one could be related to hypnosis.

area of the brain that controls automatic coordination is called the hypothalamus, and the gland ruling it the pituitary.

The brain, by all the elements of the nervous system, including those which are as yet unknown, controls even the farthest cell of the body, so as to maintain the necessary *stability* by a constant interrelation. Every stimulus we receive, one way or another, goes to the hypothalamus and this stimulus varies our stability in one *manner* or another, influencing our emotional state.

I want to emphasize that altering this stability may be conscious or not, depending on the kind or intensity of the stimulus and depending on the caliber of the brain as a capable computer. This is basic to understanding and teaching "corporal (body) expression." The empirical knowledge of the relationship between a stimulus and corporal reaction has been known since Homer, as well as its double function: *going out and coming in.*

From what has been stated so far, we see that the differences in extrasensory perception among different people could depend on the number, quality, and distribution of the sensitive neurocells and fibers of the vascular system. I should also say that the individual's practice of perceiving and emitting would be equivalent to the juggling performed by the hypothalamus and to a greater capability of the person.

To use the name thalamus for a group of very complicated nervous nuclei working as mediators to the cerebral cortex, and the name hypothalamus for the other nervous centers situated lower, or hypophysis for the gland which governs them is not at all important in a general sense. Even if they are not fully studied they would still function in their own way, no matter what we call them.

We know well enough the centers forming the hypothalamus in animals but not so much in man. Therefore, we are not scientifically prepared to make definite statements; however, manifestations of the sympathetic nervous system have been observed when there are injuries in the centers of the posterior region: sleepiness is present when the mamillary bodies in the brain are destroyed.

The mediating nuclei of the thalamus have only parasympathetic effects. But the relationships such as thalamo-hypothalamic and cortico-thalamo-hypothalamic are very important. And it is necessary to keep these in mind when explaining paranormal phenomena.

The sense organs in animals are in many cases far superior to those of men. But it is the ability to interrelate what is perceived and to use this to draw conclusions afterwards that makes the human brain more divine in nature.

An example of an acute sense in animals is that of the bat, using its built-in sonar and radar instruments to fly with undiminished speed in the dark through thin wire mesh without disturbing any of the strands of the mesh. The blackmartin, which looks like a swallow and lives like the latter in the edges of roofs, uses incredible flying curves to chase insects at twilight, picking them up with its tongue. The horse, widely opening its nostrils, seems to be receiving some kind of stimulus from afar which, because of its nature, is not susceptible to detection, appreciation, and perception by the sense of smell alone. It could very well be using other kinds of sense organs, for instance, the vascular nerve endings of the mucous membrane lining the turbinates. Some dogs can foretell their masters' death for as much as several hours in advance. Even today we are so amazed at the perceptive ability and the obedience of the dolphin. There are many such phenomena.

But let me emphasize the importance of the vascular nerve endings so as to better explain my extrasensory perception theory based on the experiences of my own life. At the age of nine I started hypnotizing animals (see *A Doctor's Odyssey*) and wound up teaching and practicing corporal expression, especially for dramatic arts students, to which I have been devoted since September, 1974.

The sensitive vascular nerve fibers are irregularly distributed throughout the different parts of the body and the number of these varies depending on the individual. We can find them among the ones that decrease the inner diameter of the arteries and arterioles (the vasoconstrictors) and among the ones that increase the lumen (internal diameter) of the blood vessels (the vasodilators.) These all have interconnections that are still very much unknown both anatomically and physiologically. However, we have been thinking for some time now that all of the nervous plexus or some part of it enervating the vascular system could be the antenna receiving the stimuli that give rise to extrasensory perceptions in the brain, and transmitting the later cerebral messages to other individuals (telepathy).

The most important arteries carrying blood to the brain are without doubt the internal carotid arteries (both right and left). At exactly their initial bifurcation, there is an enlargement known as the carotid sinus which is thoroughly lined with the endings of Hering sinusal nerves and where Fernando de Castro found a huge number of vasoconstrictor nerve fibers. Among these there were many very sensitive ones. In the same way, Dr. Isaac Costero located the nerve endings below the nails, working mainly on arterio-venous glomic anastomoses of the fingertips and toenails.

I will go a little further in the description of the neurocells of the blood vessels to give a clearer idea of my theory. We have three kinds of these cells: first, those producing dilation; second, those producing constriction; and third, the very sensitive nerve cells that contribute to the formation of the nerve fibers around the arteries, which I will call S.P. cells from this point.

When the blood vessels dilate, the fibers of the S.P. cells extend like an accordion because they need to cover a larger space. When the vessels constrict, the pleats of the accordion of nerve fibers draw closer together covering a smaller space, and it seems logical that energy can then be concentrated.

Of course, their functions vary according to the dilation and constriction of the vessels. It is doubtless that when the vessels constrict, the hypersensitive S.P. cells are able to perform as the transmitting antenna much more powerfully.

It is well known that a circle of people holding hands and concentrating on a certain thought causes reinforcement of their psychic energy. This is because of the settled integration of the engrammes in the brain of each member of the circle. And with this idea, the movement of the hypnotist's hands even behind the subject being hypnotized also takes on a new meaning, the understanding of which had been lacking before.

We could also now explain more fully the therapeutic results of massage, which, of course, depend on the person applying it. Then there are other examples such as manipulating the ouija board and blind people actually reading by using the fingers and toes, as some seers can do without using their sense of sight.

To prove this theory, it would be necessary to try out experiments similar to the ones used to prove the emission of radiation from radioactive substances: exposing photographic plates or a wave receiver to the object, using a parabolic antenna, or even a caloric-energy detector, or a micro-platismograph.

The successful instrument or system used would detect the number, quality, and location of the hypersensitive vascular neurocells in persons having the remarkable capability of performing experiments with parapsychological phenomena.

Another proof, though less defined and so less convincing, would come from a chosen group of individuals, each with great mental powers of communication, integrating their efforts to convey unspoken messages. Other similar sensitized individuals would try to receive these messages and try to indicate the kind of energy being emitted and gathered by their own antennae.

If all of this reveals positive results, we would then realize that a very well organized brain is able, by concentration, to convey a certain energy through the vascular nervous plexus, and that this energy is capable of being received by a then sensitized person whose neurovascular antenna is so stimulated to transmit the collected energy to his own brain to be reproduced as perception. It would be then that premonition, telepathy, clairvoyance, automatic writing, the ability to speak unknown languages, reading by what has been called dermovision, animal magnetism, suggestion, hypnosis, and all such paranormal phenomena become more understandable.

Before accepting this theory, though, we have to draw out the answers from human nature, demonstrating the truth of what we assume to be true. It is only after verification that there can be a basis for new advances in this very interesting, unknown, and all-encompassing area of knowledge. But even today there are still errors and abuses in trying to explain such knowledge due to a lack of objectivity.

Our main motive has been the nonaccepting attitude toward other unproven theories, and we take this same position toward our own because there is a lack of definite scientific proof. But being that there are anatomical and physiological bases for these phenomena, it would serve us well to direct experiments in this field to gather the proof we need. In the face of so many conflicting and misleading theories, we must be congruent to ourselves only and expect to encounter the means of confirming our theory.

# APPENDIX: MIND-EXPANDING LESSONS

### *Introduction*

When I presented my organic theory for ESP for the first time at the International Meeting of Parapsychologists at the Iberoamerican University in Mexico City (December 1974), some of my friends—parapsychologists, medical doctors, and Dr. Hubert Lasser, survivor of a concentration camp—advised me to design a series of lessons based on my morphological findings and my observations of neurovascular functions, with the idea that if we obtained favorable results, it would be an indirect demonstration of my organic theory.

Even though the idea seemed very logical to me, the fact that there were already too many courses, systems, lessons, exercises, and conferences offered by experts, professors, masters, and gurus, and presented as a general rule in twelve to twenty hours on a weekend, made me doubt the final results. However, I decided to investigate the positive results obtained in the abovementioned offerings.

Through that investigation I became aware that there are also longer and more extensive courses, including those on adequate diet and those that deal with individual abilities. People having completed these longer courses can be divided in three groups, according to their accomplishment. The first (about 50 percent) only acquires information. The second (30 percent), experimenting or witnessing certain paranormal phenomena, becomes scared and fearful and discontinues the investigation. The remaining group (20 percent) becomes convinced that either they have ESP, or they will be able to acquire it.

An explanation accounting for the last group is that the ones able to make progress were those who were organically gifted and were also willing to work and exercise in the proper direction. It is evident that the organ used will adequately develop, and the gifted brain will become more efficient when more positive engrammes are engraved in it.

Stimulated by these findings, I started putting together physical exercises with the proper psychical approach and the *necessary* spiritual attitude, to obtain a well-balanced influence over the neurovascular elements integrating the "antenna" and the reflexogenic zone, which connects them with the brain to develop sensibility, sensitivity, psychic ability, and ESP.

We have observed that a 21-day period is necessary for the proper installment of positive engrammes, thus the ten lessons are established for this period.

Each lesson will take two hours: one hour for information and one hour for exercises. During these lessons and exercises, the pupil should be concentrating fully on his being.

The lessons will be imparted on alternate days. In the days between lessons it is *necessary* to practice as much as possible the preceding lessons and to keep a positive attitude in the three physical, psychical, and spiritual levels. It means concentrating on the movements with a positive attitude, with the conviction that one will indeed progress and that everything will contribute to this progress—for his personal improvement, to the benefit of his fellowmen, and with the Divine Spirit's blessings.

Beyond this, the results for each pupil will be proportional to the quantity of neurovascular elements he possesses, their distribution, and their degree of complexity.

It is not strange that the number of pupils who progress in an extraordinary way is minimal. At the Second International Society for Psychical Research Conference held in Cambridge at Trinity College, March 28-30, 1978, Dr. H. Pincott proved that a very high degree of psi probability is extremely rare, although an intermediate degree of psi probability can be estimated as high as 60 percent.

That agrees with most of my findings and perhaps is comparable to what happens in artistic activities such as music, painting, Olympic gymnastics, and such. Very few people actually stand out in international challenges!

Each pupil should be advised that when he begins to feel some outstanding progress, it is important that he seek out a friend or another interested party. In this way help could be given if necessary, as it has been observed in "out of the body" experiences that accidents do happen. Of course, at the very beginning of training another person helps to correct positions and establish the proper individual rhythm, body expression, and concentration, which an individual cannot do alone.

Disciples who have been training themselves in yoga or who have been practicing transcendental meditation, or belong to the Rosicrucian Movement—even only those who have observed spontaneously paranormal phenomena—will have an advantage at the very beginning. The effort, dedication, and determination will help them to make very good progress. Failure to do so may leave them behind in relation to those of their friends with more willpower.

## LESSON ONE

We shall endeavor to become aware of the human body as a whole, rather than as various separate functioning units. However, to understand the human body and its functions, we must first examine it from different points of view and as one unit of separate parts. Our physical self is composed of many different parts. We are going to describe the three most important involved in developing psychic ability and ESP, namely the nervous, vascular, and respiratory systems. They are formed from a great variety of living cells, according to their own functions. The neuron, studied by Cajal, transmits information by means of impulses. The human body has between 12 and 20 billion neurons, but it is a fact that we only use 10 or 15 percent of them. There is a great variety of neurons with their own particular functions, but all of them are composed of a body with a nucleus and its different structures and two kinds of fibers—one that will receive impulses from other neurons, called the dendrite, and the other which transmits the impulses, called the axon.

It is a scientific fact that all the sensory cells of the body are not found in the brain. Therefore, it seems logical to search for the psychical antenna in parts of the body apart from the brain. The elements we shall describe are found in other parts of the body, but directly influence the brain, its vascularization, and its function.

The vascular system is also composed of a large variety of vascular cells. It is considered the variable support for the nerve fibers encircling the surface of the arteries in a helical formation, as discovered by Dr. Costero. Also discovered by Dr. Costero were the arterio-venous glomic anastomoses found at the base of the fingernails and toenails.

These are bundles of nerve fibers encircling the union between the arterial and venous capillaries at the base of the nails. Dr. Fernando de Castro has discovered nerve cells at the sides of the carotid sinus, and we believe that these are another component of the antenna. In the joints and cavities of the human body are found Pachionian corpuscles, more receptor units of our body and yet another component of our psychical antenna. The respiratory system is the means of supplying the necessary oxygen to these nerve cells, as well as to the rest of the body.

It should be remembered that even though we have explained these functions individually, they must be thought of as functioning as one unit. Included in this unit is a psychical element produced by the functioning body. As well as physical and psychical elements, there is also a spiritual element, and from the instant life begins that conation becomes present in a being, and these elements will begin to work in that body. Conation, which is defined as the power that directs or impels an effort of any kind, may be the most fundamental of all brain functions, the other two being cognition and feeling, and the three of them bear a great importance in the life of an individual.

In the same way that there are no two identical sets of fingerprints, there are no two identical brains, or beings, and, equally so, the components of the antenna, i.e., the nerve fibers encircling the arteries. The bundles in the arterio-venous anastomoses, the nerve cells of the carotid sinuses, vary not only in the number and distribution but also in quality, as observed by the electron microscope.

One concept that must be realized is that although the brain governs the body and its functions, the brain, in turn, is governed by the information it receives from all parts of the body or from whatever sensory input reaches it through the antenna.

## The Habit of Concentration

The art of concentration can be learned and practiced in exactly the same way as any other activity. The more you practice, the more it will become a habit, as are most of our activities, and the more it becomes a habit, the more it will be developed. Concentration means focusing all our attention to an object, an item of business, or such. Total attention is necessary to prevent our mind from wandering in any other direction; there must not be the slightest deviation in thought. It is necessary to visualize, think, and concentrate all our attention upon whatever we wish.

Start by concentrating on a Ping-Pong ball crossing back and forth over a black velvet square. We need to be particularly aware of avoiding any other thought; if this occurs we must begin again. After practicing with an object like a Ping-Pong ball, and when the ability to concentrate is stronger within us, our exercises should go to a more complicated object, to a concept, to a more complicated concept, and then to a truth. However, we must be very honest with ourselves. Once the ability to concentrate is acquired, all our problems will be seen with more clarity. When your work gives good results, you do not become tired; in fact, a feeling of happiness and well-being fills your personality. What tires us is the inability to solve the problems we face. This causes insufficient conation, lack of motivation, and selfishness.

At this point, students should change into leotards for exercises which will help establish a meaningful connection between the mind and body. The students should be aware of the necessity of proper breathing and how to utilize air reserve.

1. In a relaxed standing position, shake the hands. Now raise the arms to shoulder height, still shaking the hands. Open the arms, then return them to the side of the body. Now lift one foot a few inches and shake it, repeating the arm movements; repeat, shaking the other foot. This will increase the circulation in the arterio-venous glomic anastomoses at the base of the fingernails and toenails.

2. In a relaxed standing position, concentrate on the top of your head. Now shift concentration to the muscles of the neck, moving them slightly as your concentration becomes focused on these muscles. Follow down the shoulders, arms, elbows, through the whole body, like water flowing from the top of the head to the fingertips and toes. Now reverse the flow of concentration, from the toes up to the fingers to the top of the head.

These exercises should be performed every day before the following exercises are performed. The first day, the students will perform concentration exercises, dwelling on the muscles and the harmonious posturing of the body.

## LESSON TWO

### Reception and Recipient (Vasodilation)

After many years of studying ESP, there still is no scientific explanation. In Yogic theory, the human being is present in all places simultaneously. The yogis claim to have all kinds of powers and knowledge, but they add that to achieve this, they have had special training. They admit, however, that when an organic theory about ESP is proven, all the previous concepts about telepathy and other phenomena will have to be revised.

The Rosicrucians believe that a center for perception does exist for everyone, dreams, hypnosis, and inspiration being the way for many people to experience perception. Dr. Douglas Dean has observed, with the use of the platismograph, the existence of blood-volume variations associated with emotional responses, and that the same phenomena occur when emotional disturbance is produced by telepathy.

It has been said that a hypnotized subject can often taste the food that the hypnotist is tasting, or describe the object that the hypnotist is holding in his hand.

The personality traits that are characteristic of a good recipient are: good nature, self-confidence, enthusiasm, alertness, good emotional temperament, a realistic outlook, flexibility in responses, and composure, and a relaxed nature.

Relaxation can be obtained by concentrating or by directing thought; when excessive tension exists, it is necessary to have the help of a master in this case.

The personality traits of the sender are: a pleasant personality, the ability to feel fear and yet control it, a faith and willingness to accomplish lifetime goals, self-confidence, quick tempered yet able to control it, maximum sensory awareness, an extraordinary intellect, mental and physical vigor, and a sense of having a mission to perform, with an identity seeking unity and oneness.

We all have doubts and fears, worries and preoccupations, and these disturbances limit our activities and our ability to think; conversely, action eliminates preoccupations and doubts.

Students should write down a list of their worries, fears, and preoccupations. Each should seal them in an envelope, and the teacher should discuss them either publicly or privately at the end of these lessons.

Frustrations and failures should be an incentive to try again in a better way. If you have made progress in your concentration exercises, it is advisable to now concentrate on planning for the unexpected with a realistic attitude. The result of success in these exercises up to now will be to prepare you to receive telepathic messages, premonitions, and hunches, and perhaps to receive something of the universal knowledge.

in the different aspects, forms, or facets. These exercises are not only for the physical part of our body, but also for the psychical and spiritual. Every new movement with the proper concentration and the correct attitude may be opening thousands of brain capillaries at the time that new engrammes are established. As the three parts grow gradually the individual will develop according to the number of cells and fibers he possesses.

In the spiritual part it is important to keep in mind the use of good taste and originality, and to project from our body the part we want to be more noticeable. We must think of what we are doing, and do what we are thinking. We must devote ourselves wholly to a task we are performing, in mind and body. If we are doing something good, legitimate, and honest, it is easy to convince, conquer, and persuade. We need to throw away our negative thinking, pessimism, and sadness, and in time we shall be able to direct our thoughts to any part of our body, sending our energies through it (for example, acupuncture), and later on our ideas can be sent to any place we wish. Plato said that ideas exist as visible thought forms. The aura can be hurt or damaged, and perhaps our dress and clothing interfere with our aura.

The students should change into leotards for exercises.

By this time, the students have already become conscious of the volume of their body; they have mobilized all their joints and muscles which before were used unconsciously and are now being used consciously.

After doing some warm-up exercises:

1. Perform some previous exercises, selecting those that the students found more difficult.

2. In a relaxed standing position, imagine how your body expands to occupy the space of your physical aura (two inches larger all around). The arms should swing out, legs should be apart, the head held up. Now feel the same with your eyes closed and start walking. At first you can walk in a circle, opening the eyes once in a while to reassure yourself but closing them again. Concentrate on feeling the aura, and from this try not to hit anything or anyone. New engrammes will be formed concerning

your idea about the aura. At home, the students should do exercises to enrich the five senses, for example, observation of colors, animals, people, but should not daydream. Concentrate on reasoning out the actions of various animals, objects, and such.

## LESSON FOUR

This lesson deals with the process of thinking, influence and silent induction, organic silence, and psychic power.

*The process of thinking.* To think is to meditate and in order to make a decision we must meditate. To think in the past is to remember and in the future to predict. The ability to think is what differentiates man from other animals. We should make an effort to read with the mind. According to Sigmund Freud, all neuroses are a consequence of sexual repression, and the means to get rid of these repressions is obtained through sublimation, and by the mechanism of transference, the neuroses can be cured. We can, by sublimation, obtain a transference from sexual power to mind power. Sexual energy, when strong and not channeled through art or some other outlet, may show itself in sexual neuroses or deviations. It is more convenient to channel it into mental power.

*Influence and silent induction.* This psychic power, when developed through concentration, can be used to establish contact with other people and manifest sympathy in them and for them; it is then possible to establish an empathic coupling, detectable with Kirlian photography. Alternatively, it can be used for silent induction; that is, the influencing of another person's physical feelings to make him perform a routine physical act without his being aware of doing anything extraordinary.

*Organic silence.* When an individual relives one of his past experiences so completely as to become unaware of his surroundings, his body enters a state of organic silence, and any radiation that was previously emitted with his train of thought then will be radiated again, through his astral aura, to be received by anyone capable of doing so.

*Psychic Power.* The existence of individuals with more psychic power than others is undeniable. However, we should be aware that the musician, the artist, the poet, the scientist, and the philosopher also have particular power in their respective fields. So psychic power can be developed, especially if it will be used for beneficial purposes. It should be used with modesty, honesty, and without presumption. Using psychic power for evil is equivalent to suicide. It is necessary at this point to become aware of the psychic-physical-spiritual unity and the engrammes interconnecting them, and from this we may understand the mechanism of phenomena that were not previously explainable.

Circulatory changes at the base of the fingernails as observed with the platismograph, and the peripheral vessels and even in the brain (my two cases, 1949) may have a direct relation to psychic phenomena.

Students should change into leotards for exercises.

After warm-up exercises and repetition of those exercises found to be more difficult for the students:

1. Students are placed in two rows facing each other, with one arm behind the back, the feet in a stable position, and the other arm joined to the person facing so as to arm wrestle; do so in a gentle manner.

2. Send all the energy from the brain to the hand, leaving the rest of the body in complete relaxation. Repeat the exercise.

3. With concentration and full attention, repeat the exercises with the other hand. Now the students should form a circle.

4. Relax and breathe deeply, and suspend one hand in front of the eyes and concentrate on making a fist, leaving the body as relaxed as possible. Concentrating, open and close the hand again. Now open the hand, finger by finger, and make a fist, closing the hand finger by finger. The rest of the body must be completely relaxed. Repeat with the other hand.

By this time, the students should have supple muscles and a feeling of their corporal dimensions. They should realize that we pay all this attention to the body in the beginning in order to be able to forget about the body later.

5. With the eyes closed, touch the left ear with the right hand and vice versa several times.

6. With eyes closed, feel the motion of the facial muscles, concentrating first on the chin, trying to move it; then move the eyebrows together, then separate them. Move the bridge of the nose muscle then the nostrils. Then move the tongue around the space between the lips and gums, first clockwise, then counter-clockwise.

7. Now push the tongue as hard against one cheek as possible, push back with the cheek, and vice versa with the other cheek.

We should perform these movements with maximum concentration and attention, imagining ourselves to be in a movie, creating an atmosphere of an execution. We should realize that we imagine the reality, and we fantasize the imaginary, and the former is the important thing we must do. Imaginary things have no place here.

## LESSON FIVE

### Sensitive Zones of the Body

It is well known that the body has different sensory zones; for example the erogenous zones (the earlobe, elbow, neck) and the hypnotic zones. There are also zones that are sensitive to the stare of an observer, and all these zones are more sensitive depending on the person who provokes them. Explorers of the sensitive zones will find different amounts of sensitivity, depending on the explorer as well as the subjects; and this difference in individual response can be detected and studied now by Kirlian photography. These responses are due to reflex reactions, the mechanism of some of them being unknown. Thus we can now explain how acupuncture and faith healing by the laying on of hands work, and also how pain can be removed, but in a transitory form.

We should avoid physical or mental exhaustion and stop before we get too tired; we should be completely relaxed and breathe deeply. Never rush to accomplish a task, and realize that all beginnings are not only hard but also slow, as you are not only acquiring new engrammes, but may be opening some of the blind capillaries in the mute areas of your brain which will become useful later. This process, however, takes time.

The students should change into leotards and have an orange with them.

After warm-up exercises:

1. Each student should sit with the orange in his hands, in order to test the sixth sense. Examine the orange visually, carefully, every square inch, looking for fine details on the surface. Also be aware of the texture of the orange. When the visual and physical examination is completed, close your eyes and, through touch, visualize the fine detail that was previously observed until a full image appears in our perception. Now feel the orange with the palms of the hands, with the forearm, the forehead, the face, the chin, the eyelids, the nose. As it passes the nose, smell the aroma and see if it varies in different parts of the orange.

Now begin to peel the orange, trying to keep the peel in one piece, continually smelling and feeling the orange as you peel. When part of the peel is separated, place the orange close to the ear, to hear the sound of the orange being peeled. Use both ears to find which ear hears the orange better; listen to hear whether the orange says anything to you. Try to imagine what the orange is feeling. Return the orange to your nose frequently to see if the smell varies.

Rest the peel on your lap and feel the texture of the peeled orange. Feel the difference between peeled and unpeeled. Very carefully remove the pith from the orange in small pieces, hearing and smelling the orange. Now that the orange is completely peeled, it will become a crystal ball in your hands; look deeply into it with your mind and see what the crystal ball may show or tell you. This will take more or less time depending on the individual student.

When this stage is finished, eat the orange slowly, savoring the different tastes of this fruit, trying to taste as many as possible.

When each student leaves, he should retain the image of the

orange as vividly as possible, and when he arrives home, he should write down a total description of the orange test, and bring it for the sixth lesson.

## LESSON SIX

This lesson will show you how to use only the necessary energy to accomplish a task, avoiding a cortical blockage—using telepathy.

An interesting case deals with an actress in a play called "The Exorcism." After much applause from the audience after the play ended, the actress died on the stage. This could have been avoided if she had used only part of her brain, and dilated the blood vessels on one side; this could be considered a form of involuntary autohypnosis.

About hypnosis we know the effects and we study the results, but the real causes that produce it are unknown.* The involuntary autohypnosis and the cortical blockage are consequences of the unknown mechanism that produces the hypnosis but are not their causes. This can be prevented by the person who knows the other mechanism of the brain, mainly the circulatory process. The most important physical symptom of hypnosis is that the blood goes to the periphery of the body, leaving the brain less irrigated. Psychically this lack of enough blood over the central nervous system may alter the vegetative, the sympathetic, and the parasympathetic, and the nerve cells and nerve fibers which use the vascular system as a support may be less active.

From the spiritual view, hypnosis begins in an induction zone in which a nerve plexus is located. This may explain why those who try to achieve an out-of-the-body experience put themselves in grave danger. It is also necessary to take great care to avoid the possible consequences of exaggerated mental efforts, as they can also provoke cortical blockage.

*In this book, we haxe exposed our view of the different stages of hypnosis and how they may be produced.

We should not only use but also be very aware of the necessary effort and not expend more than the necessary energy that is needed in any case. We should also realize that different tasks require different amounts of energy.

Our exercises should be directed in such a way that tension only appears in those parts we are using, and the rest of our body should be completely relaxed. It requires a lot of training and concentration. The amplification of a given sense (hyperacusia) should always be performed under the supervision of a qualified person, at least until the apprentice has learned the techniques.

At home the student should rest, relax, perceive imaginary odors, listen to imaginary music, imagine his native village, and so on in order to advance.

The students should change into leotards for exercises.

The exercises you are learning to perform may be somewhat similar to any of the 840,000 yoga exercises, but the most valuable is to visualize your movements because this is even more important than doing them. To establish a meaningful connection between mind and body with the proper attitude is essential and, remember, that by deep breathing a vital energy force is acquired; breathe only through the nose, alternating your concentration from one nostril to the other.

1. In a standing position, imagine that the head is separated from the neck, but resting on it with perfect equilibrium. Relax neck muscles, placing only the weight of the head on cervical vertebrae. All tension is relieved from the whole body. With your mind, feel all the parts of the body. The teacher should correct posture and nonrelaxed sections of students' bodies by light touch only. Breathe deeply, slowly inhale and exhale.

2. Feel your body's weight; try to diminish it; make the body as light as possible. Now do the reverse and walk clockwise and counterclockwise, becoming lighter until you almost float. Rest and breathe deeply. With eyes closed, make yourself smaller and smaller. Return to normal. Then make yourself taller and larger. Rest again.

Feel your whole body while doing the exercises, feeling and

imagining simultaneously. At this time the students should have already acquired enough knowledge about their own bodies and about enlarging their sensibility, which goes hand in hand with the degree of sensitivity and extrasensory perception. This is because of the unity of the human body. The general idea that a low IQ means higher psychic powers is not true; in fact, as a man becomes educated he can start to use his powers according to his will, rather than occasionally, without direction.

## LESSON SEVEN

### MIND OVER MATTER, LEVITATION, FANTASTIC REALITIES

The concept of mind over matter is a very old one. During the Middle Ages, a Jewish countryman of mine, born in Cordoba in 1135, and named Moses ben Maimon (later Maimonides) wrote in Arabic the *Guide of the Perplexed*. He was very much against corruption and degeneration, and he became involved in the workings of high virtues and influences from the celestial sphere and how they effected and modified matter. Admitting that the human soul was originated as a force in the celestial sphere, he even felt that the power of the mind, if it was directed toward divination, could predict many occurrences.

It is understandable that a mind-over-matter influence could produce levitation. We are aware that barbiturates and psychedelic drugs sometimes make some users feel that they are weightless. With the proper exercises, you will not only acquire a weightless feeling, but your walk will be lighter and more graceful, and though not all of you will levitate or feel very light, eventually someone will discover that he has the power to levitate.

Levitation is the inexplicable elevation of a human body or an object, in the presence of a medium or a group of people, by the means of psychical effects, without any physical intervention. Levitation is known from older times; in Sanskrit it was defined as the extranatural power to make oneself very light at will. Buddhism admits levitation, and in 233 A.D., Iamblichus elevated himself ten cubits from the ground when preaching. Many saints, like Joseph in Italy (1603-1663), ascended into the air in front of an audience of believers.

In 1874 Daniel D. Home elevated himself more than a hundred times in front of scientists who witnessed the fact and who described Home as being in a trance. Many fakers present themselves on stage and at private parties, as was the case of Robert Odin. In today's exercises practice will be very important because we need to put into practice all that we have learned and acquired. We will try, by concentrating on ourselves, to make our bodies float in the air by means of a force created by us and in imaginary surroundings (sky, garden, lake, or sea). This exercise could be improved if we shine blue light over the students, but they must be so relaxed that no tensions, worries, or preoccupations carry over from everyday life or from recent events. Any effect obtained through drugs (LSD, barbiturates, stimulants, and such) can be duplicated by the proper use of this system.

Students should change into leotards for exercises.

Most of our exercises today need to be tied up to the imagination and to use the memory of the emotions.

1. In the cobra position, bring your hands to the sides of the body, raise the head and shoulders, looking forward. Look right and left in a snake-like fashion. From this posture, change to the cat position. Return to the cobra position.

2. Exercises of attention, coordination, belief, faith, and reality by means of concentration and imagination follow. Play volleyball without a ball. Observe rhythm, and the muscular tensions which must be eliminated. All the exercises should be performed with eyes closed first, then opened.

## LESSON EIGHT

### Reincarnation or Extracerebral Memory—Metempsychosis

The passing of a soul from one body to another after death is a very old belief, with religious and philosophical implications.

It was born in the Orient and is now popular in the West. The belief contends that the soul transmigrates after death according to what occurred in the previous life. Some countries have different versions of the belief, though they are basically the same.

The early followers of Judaism did not believe in this transmigration of the soul, but with the Cabala this belief became more accepted.

There are two recent cases—one in Madhya Pradesch, India, and the other in Philadelphia, Pennsylvania—which may establish reincarnation as a fact. In the first case, a young Indian girl recognized friends and relatives from a previous life she lived in a village she had never visited. Dr. Ian Stevenson, of the University of Virginia, found that out of forty-nine statements made by the girl concerning details of her previous life, only two were incorrect. The girl recalled the disease from which she died, as well as the doctor who treated her. She also recalled incidents that could only be known to her in a previous life.

The case in America involved a woman who, under hypnosis, claimed to be a Swedish peasant, and she could speak Swedish fluently. She was able to identify objects brought from the American-Swedish Historical Museum in Philadelphia, and research showed there was no opportunity for her to have learned Swedish in her present life.

H. N. Baneryce calls "extracerebral memory" reincarnation. I mentioned the case in Bahçe of the farmer who was murdered. A few months later a boy was born in a nearby village, and when the boy was older, he returned to his prior life—the village (where the other man was killed some years prior), and was able to recognize most of the man's relatives and friends.

Having an interest in psychic phenomena may be the first sign of being a sender or a recipient. I have in my own experience found persons who were not mediums but thought of themselves as a computer or as a channel tuned into a universal mind in a subconscious fashion. The idea behind it is that one's deeds in a previous life shaped or prepared the new body for the present life, giving a desirable universality. Through a series of regressions it was revealed that one woman lived four previous lives, the first one fifteen to thirty years before the birth of Christ.

Students should change into leotards.

The exercises in this lesson consist of observing animals, identifying with them, and after establishing a rapport with one that has been selected, not to imitate it, but to become that animal. The new engrammes created in this exercise will be advantageous to the student later.

## LESSON NINE

By now we have acquired a large amount of concentration, sensitivity, and sensibility. We must realize that with perseverance the questions *what, where, why, who* will find deeper answers. Our brain has new engrammes, and new capillaries have been opened by the engrammes. By channeling our energy, our antenna is now more developed and ready to work, and this is a step forward. We should not think about bad luck. I am firmly convinced that talent and ability always find their own level. It is not in doing what we like to do, but in liking what we do, where the secret of happiness lies. Complete security does not exist. To do something better than average takes ability, and ability takes us inevitably to success.

Mistakes and errors should be accepted as lessons, and when you reach the point of being a master, you will no longer remember the failures and disappointments; this is all part of the learning process. As always this will take time and effort, but the reward will justify this effort. It is my belief that now you have learned with your own effort, you can make your own predictions, and see how well you do. Organizing your new engrammes with the previous ones will give new concepts that will again form new engrammes, and will furnish you with new sources of energy to be sent out through your antenna, making it more effective.

Students should change into leotards. Exercise at will. The instructor will lead the group through the most advisable exercises according to their needs.

## LESSON TEN

We shall deal in this last lesson with kindness and beauty, Karmic laws and sexual energy.

We have developed in ourselves powers that bring us closer to God. In our hours of sleep, we not only rest, but we detoxicate our aura, being in a very receptive state, and perform subconscious work that we will utilize while awake. This will have a different effect on each of us. Homeostasis and conation are unique in every person.

Beauty, which is actually the end of every work of the learned person, is eternal, and everything beautiful participates in universal beauty. This beauty is also good, so beauty and kindness are like two rays of supreme light, melted as one when they reach the proper degree of sublimation. Beauty in itself is divine and elevates the soul and makes it more noble. Beautiful aesthetics will imply image and emotion, and aesthetic expression and communication will make us not only better people, full of kindness, but also more beautiful, and we shall project both to our friends, acquaintances, and even passersby.

Through my theory and this system we may enlarge and enrich our sixth sense, feeling more subtle "vibrations" with our antenna, and so gain a greater sense of beauty.

The Karmic laws or law of cause and effect should always be kept in mind, especially when we have acquired this new force, which could be used for either good or evil; however, the use of this new force for evil will not only destroy the newly acquired power but also destroy the personality of the user.

Students should change into leotards for exercises. The following exercises should be done first with the eyes closed, later with the eyes opened.

1. Creating beauty and kindness with our body requires not only attention and concentration but humility, naturalness, and an aesthetic internal feeling implying a great concept of beauty, or "I am beautiful," and feeling slowly an inner perception of

conviction and truth. The inner feeling is not only the engine of our emotions but the source of our power, will, mind, or whatever you want to call it. If we concentrate on what we are creating and we allow it to flow from us as light from a candle, we will emit beauty and kindness.

2. In this exercise concentrate on kindness. Hold an idea of universal love of everything, and make an effort to project it with your eyes, hips, and all your being. Relax, and start again.